674

C000255728

Walks in the
Ancient Peak District

Robert Harris

Published by Sigma Leisure – an imprint of
Sigma Press, 5 Alton Road, Wilmslow, Cheshire SK9 5DY, England.

British Library Cataloguing in Publication Data
A CIP record for this book is available from the British Library.

ISBN: 1-85058-822-8

Typesetting and Design by: Sigma Press, Wilmslow, Cheshire.

Cover photographs: main picture, The Bullstones; bottom row, left to right: Arbor Low, Nine Stones Close, Wincle Minn Standing Stones *(all photographs by Robert Harris)*

Maps and illustrations: Robert Harris. Maps reproduced from Ordnance Survey mapping on behalf of The Controller of Her Majesty's Stationery Office. © Crown Copyright. Licence Number MC 100032058

Printed by: Bell & Bain Ltd, Glasgow

Disclaimer: the information in this book is given in good faith and is believed to be correct at the time of publication. No responsibility is accepted by either the author or publisher for errors or omissions, or for any loss or injury howsoever caused. Only you can judge your own fitness, competence and experience.

Preface

This is a book of walks which visit the sites and monuments left to us by the prehistoric people of the Peak District. The first people to reach this area were the Stone Age hunters of the Ice Age who followed the herds of bison and reindeer as they migrated north in the brief arctic summers. They found temporary shelter in the deep limestone gorges and caves of the White Peak. Over thousands of years the climate warmed and in the spreading forests a growing number of hunters and gatherers lived on the plants and animals they found around them. Then came farming and for the first time people became settled. They cleared the woods, tilled the land and grazed their animals on the higher heaths and moors.

These people were the first to build structures that still survive to this day. Their great henges and stone circles, standing stones and burial mounds can still be found scattered across the spectacular hills and valleys of the Peak, often linked by ancient trackways that can still be followed.

The walks in this book vary in length from as little as four miles to some of almost ten. They also vary in difficulty, some following the quiet lanes and well-marked footpaths of the White Peak, while others climb up onto the bleak heaths and edges of the higher gritstone moors.

Each walk visits sites that help us to understand more about the way of life of these, our ancient ancestors, who lived in this wonderful area before the coming of the Romans. Some visit their tombs, others their places of worship, while some climb up to their settlements and forts perched high on isolated hills. Some visit the secret caves deep beneath ground where strange and unexplained rituals were carried out.

I have divided the book into four sections, the White Peak with its limestone plateau and deep-cut dales, and the three areas of high gritstone moorland which surround it. I have called these the Dark Peak, the East Moors and the Western Moors of Cheshire and Staffordshire.

All the routes are circular, most starting and finishing in a town or village that is easy to locate and convenient to reach by car. They pass through some of the finest scenery in England and all are worthwhile in themselves, but I hope that the historical element included not only adds interest, but also gives a focus to each of the walks.

When taking the higher level walks, always follow the usual rules of mountain safety. Go properly equipped, always carry a map and compass and know how to use them. Be prepared for sudden and dramatic changes in the weather. When visiting the many caves mentioned in the walks remember that exploration of any cave system is potentially dangerous and should only be attempted by those who are suitably experienced.

The maps in this book are sketch maps only. For greater detail and accuracy consult the appropriate O.S. Outdoor Leisure or Landranger sheet. The walks follow public rights of way, and many of them are on land now designated as 'Access Land', but some remain on private land. Treat all property with respect and if in doubt, always ask permission.

Equally importantly, respect these ancient and sacred sites, which in many cases have survived for over five thousand years. They are our link with our history and a precious window into our past. Treat them with the respect they deserve and help to preserve them for future generations to appreciate.

Lastly I would like to express my gratitude to the following people, without whom the writing of this book would have been a much more difficult, and not nearly so enjoyable an experience. Mairi, Howard and Graham for their much-appreciated company on the walks, and Bethan and Rowenna for accompanying me into the deepest depths of Foxhole Cave. John and Norma Needham for their invaluable assistance, especially with the history of cave exploration in the Peak District. Dan Robinson at the Grosvenor Museum in Chester for his help in identifying artifacts, and Paul Mortimer and the staff at the South Peak Estate office for their help in finding and accessing some of the ancient caves located on National Trust land. Finally, my wife Mairi for tirelessly proof-reading all my writing, Bethan for her critical assistance with the sketches, and the staff at Sigma Press for their much appreciated support.

Bob Harris

Dedication
For Mairi

Contents

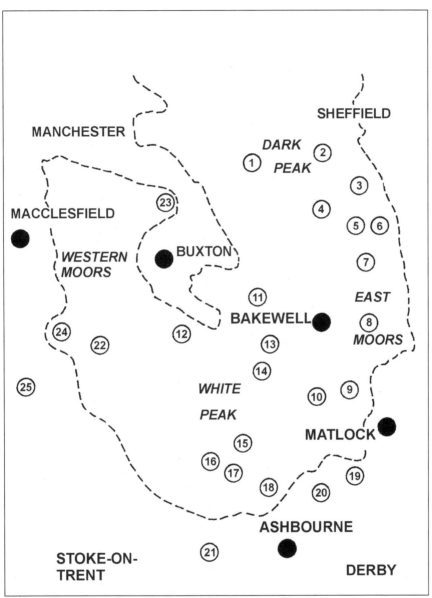

Locations of Walks

Key to symbols used on maps

◊	Standing Stone
♠♠	Stone Circle
♠♠	Ring Cairn
△	Cairn or Tumulus
◁	Long Cairn
⌂	Burial Chamber
⌇⌇	Enclosure
⋙	Defensive Banks and Ditches
℮	Carved Stones
⅀	Rock Shelters
⌒	Caves
♭	Ancient Spring or Well
⊟	Natural Rock Feature
⋙	Cliffs
⋇	Marsh
⌒⌒	Lake or Reservoir
+	Church

Introduction

Rising up above the plains of lowland England, the low hills of the Peak District have always stood out as a land apart. Its rocky plateau stands like a raised shelf above the level plains stretching away to the east, west and south, but below the high and inhospitable moors to the north. It is shaped very much like a bowl, with a central limestone plateau ringed by higher gritstone moors on all sides, except to the south where instead, it falls gradually away towards the valley of the Trent. Its limestone heart, the White Peak, is cut through by a number of rivers which drain southwards down narrow and steep-sided dales to join their parent river.

For hundreds of thousands of years this landscape would have been submerged beneath the great ice sheets which blanketed much of northern England. In the brief interludes when the climate warmed and the ice retreated, the land would have greened. Great herds of bison and reindeer would have migrated northwards each year following the summer sun.

It is quite possible that it was during one of these interglacial periods, possibly as long as 500 000 years ago, that man first reached as far north as the Peak and settled, however briefly, in its sheltered valleys and caves. But each time the ice returned, driving both the hunters and their prey back to the warmer south once again, and leaving northern England devoid of all human life.

But then, the last Ice Age began to wane in about 12 000 BC, and man returned to the north, and this time he was to stay. These were a new race of man, possibly descended from the earlier hunters, but now unmistakably modern man, our own direct ancestors. They too spread from the south, over what is now the English Channel but was then just open grasslands stretching between low chalk cliffs. They came with the animals that they depended on, following the migrating herds on their long seasonal journeys.

These people have left little sign of their passing in the Peak, just a few skillfully crafted blades of stone, some rudimentary tools and the butchered bones of their meals in a few of the many sheltered caves and rock shelters which abound in its deep-sided valleys.

Just a short distance to the east, however, near the village of Cresswell, where a steep-sided limestone gorge runs through a line of low hills, there is evidence that gives us a much broader picture of the lives of these people. There, amongst the bones of bison and reindeer, mammoth and woolly rhino, wild horse and arctic fox are the remains left by the hunters who stalked them. Their diet was largely meat and they used skins for clothes. They made tools from bone as well as the hard stone, which was sometimes brought from far outside the area. They also created art, carvings and paintings that had no obvious practical use, but which must have served a purpose beyond our modern understanding. They carved horses heads out of ribs and carefully worked antlers with strange geometric patterns. Most amazingly of all are the recently discovered rock paintings, showing complex patterns, life-like images of birds and a beautiful ibex, which were not even to be found in the region. Discovered deep within the caves, these faint images are the most northerly rock art ever found from this early period and are the only examples so far recorded in Britain.

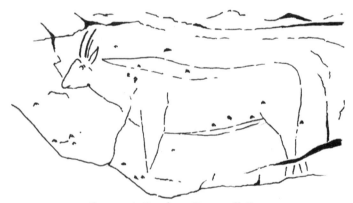

Cave painting from Cresswell Crags

What does all this tell us about these early people? It shows us that they possessed skills that they employed for more than mere survival and held complex beliefs that are now lost to us. They travelled widely and were influenced by events and cultures beyond their own territories. They almost certainly lived in large family groups, spoke a complex language and were adept at creating the fire upon which their survival in the harsh conditions depended.

For thousands of years the numbers of these people would have been relatively small, possibly no more than a few hundred people spread across the whole country. Then as the Ice Age finally drew to a close, the glaciers retreated into the northern mountains and the summers lengthened. The bare open slopes of the tundra sprouted with new life, and gradually, the land became green once more. Oak and willow and birch woodland spread over the valleys and coasts, and grasses and heather carpeted the lower hills. With the trees came different animals, spreading northwards. Bears, wolves, deer, wild cattle and pigs flourished in the new forests and with them came people in ever increasing numbers, spreading northwards up the river valleys and open plains of southern Britain.

By about 6 000 BC the melting ice had caused the sea to rise sufficiently to cut Britain off from the continent. The rising temperatures had also allowed the hunters and gatherers of this Mesolithic period to have spread to all but the most inhospitable northern mountains. In the area of the Peak, evidence in the form of stone tools made and used by these Mesolithic hunters have been found in great numbers. Sometimes in caves, but more often scattered over the light soils of the limestone hills and valleys of the White Peak.

These people would probably have lived in groups of about thirty people, loosely linked by kinship who lived by hunting the animals and collecting the seasonal fruits of the forest.

It is probable that the hunting parties would have been mostly young men, while the women and the children would have been responsible for the collecting of what fruit and nuts and roots were locally available. The old would have been supported and cared for, but would also have had their role within the group, possible looking after the very young and the sick. They would have spoken a complex language, which would have allowed them to discuss and question and express feelings. Their dead were honoured and buried with dignity.

Their lives would still have revolved around the animals they hunted, but the ever-spreading woodlands would have brought about a different way of life. No longer did the woodland animals have to travel vast distances in search of seasonal food as did the great herds of the open tundra. They could now stay and survive within the confines of the forest, moving to new grazing with ease. This allowed the hunters to stay within their own familiar territories, where they could hunt or collect all the food that they needed for their group.

From this stability would have come the beginnings of a sense of place, of belonging to an area and an understanding of it and an attachment to it. Their camps would still have moved through the year, up onto the heaths and moors in summer, down into the woods in winter and they would have known where the fruit and berries could be found and at what times of the year.

As they settled into their territories, they would have begun, very gradually, to adapt and change the landscape around them. Paths would slowly form between seasonal camps and to water sources. Evidence suggests that some of the ancient tracks running across the southern Peak have been in use for at least 7 000 years.

They would have cleared areas of woodland around their temporary settlements, cutting down the larger trees and burning off the lighter scrub. It would not have taken long to notice that old clearings used in previous years allowed the grasses to grow and that this better grazing attracted the animals on which they depended. From that, it was only a short step to actively clearing patches of woodland to entice their prey to where they could be more easily killed. They would have noticed that discarded seeds grew where they were dropped and that useful plants and trees could be encouraged to grow where they were most needed.

Over time, a social memory would have slowly developed. Certain places would have become associated with certain events. A clearing might have been known for a great hunt, a stream for a terrible accident and a tree for the fire from the sky in a great storm. Some places might have become linked with happy events and others feared as places to avoid. These places might even have taken on some responsibility for the events which occurred there, and that some things happened because of the place where they happened!

These initial superstitions must have been the first stirrings of religion, which would come to influence the lives of the people of this land for thousands of years to come.

Slowly, slowly, over time, the landscape became more than just a source of food. It became a home, a place to live, a place to be responsible for, a place to respect and a place to worship.

It is possible that certain natural features came to have greater significance than others. The notch in the hill out of which the Sun rose or set, the spring where endless pure water bubbled out of the ground or the dark cave where their ancestors had lived. It is quite likely that even old trees, which to the people of the time would have seemed almost as permanent as the rocks and streams, became places where people met and ceremonies took place.

What is certain is that even thousands of years later, monuments were still being built beside these natural features, showing that their importance remained in the social memory and that a feeling of respect continued for these very special places. It is almost certain that the stone circle of Nine Stones Close was sited below the natural rocks of Robin Hood's Stride because this was already a place of significance to the local people.

It is not clear quite how farming first arrived in the Peak, whether it was brought by new people coming from the south, or that the concept was simply adopted by the native population. Probably it was a combination of the two, but what is certain is that by about 4 500 BC it had reached southern England and had reached the Peak by about 4 000 BC.

It was most likely a gradual process, adapting an existing way of life that was already managing the surrounding wild plants and animals. Cattle, sheep and pigs began to be domesticated and wheat and beans cultivated in specially cleared areas on the light soils of the White Peak. Hunting, fishing and gathering would still have remained important as a way of supplementing their basic diet. It would have been during the next thousand years that these early Neolithic farmers became settled and farms took the place of territories.

Quite why the area of the White Peak became a centre of a New Stone

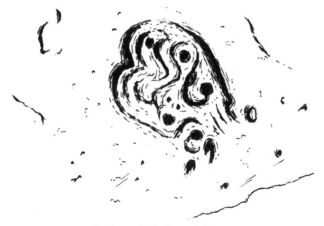

Rock symbols from Ashover

Age society can only be guessed at but it is almost certainly because of its unique geography. The fact that there were large areas of lightly wooded and easily farmed, fertile soil must have been the prime reason, but other factors such as a plentiful source of usable stone and a history of habitation trailing back into the mists of time might also have been important.

What do we know of this society? Until the coming of farming little would have been built that still remains to be seen today, but with the coming of settled farming communities came the first surviving structures. These were tombs, or barrows, built to bury the dead. They varied in size and shape from area to area but were all for communal use. Usually a chamber was constructed of large upright blocks of stone covered with even larger capping stones. This was then buried within a mound of smaller stones or earth. Many that remain in the Peak are longbarrows with a chamber only at one end. Some of these are of amazing size, Long Low being well over 200 metres long, and the now-vanished barrow at the Bridestones reputedly reached over 100 metres in length. Others are round in shape, and have more than one chamber, each entered through a separate entrance, such as at Minninglow and Ringham Low.

The chambers were usually entered through a low passage, which was opened and closed as the tomb continued to be used. Inside the tombs the bones of many individuals have often been found, not separately interred, but jumbled up inside. It is also thought likely that the dead were exposed to the elements first as few whole skeletons have been found within them, and in some chambers certain bones such as thigh bones and skulls were missing, suggesting that these were perhaps of a symbolic importance and were used for ceremonies outside the tomb.

Many of these early barrows had an open space, sometimes paved, outside the entrance. These areas, known as forecourts, are believed to be where ceremonies took place as a part of the interment.

All this tells us that this was a society that honoured its dead, and that even after death, ancestors were still revered and played a continuing role in the life of those remaining. The dissembling of the bones and the mixing together of the skeletons could well mean that the dead were no longer seen as individuals but had become a part of a communal concept, thought of simply as 'the ancestors'.

What is interesting is that these ancient places of burial continued to be used and revered for several thousand years, later cultures and societies often returning to use the tombs of their forefathers. This continuing theme of certain places being of special significance seems to run right through the prehistory of all these ancient cultures.

The very earliest of these megalithic chambers were built in Brittany, the tomb at Kercado being the oldest so far dated at around 4 800 BC, but by soon after 4 000 BC the practice had spread to southern England and the great longbarrows of the Marlborough Downs were constructed. The earliest of the Peak District barrows were probably built just a few hundred years later.

Contemporary with these early places of burial, were massive enclosures or causewayed camps. These were encircled with banks and ditches with many entrances and could have been used as trading places as well as seasonal settlements and ceremonial centres. Again, the best examples of these camps can be found in the vicinity of Marlborough Downs, Windmill Hill being the most famous example. In the Peak District, just on the dip slope of Gardom's Edge, there are the remains of a large enclosure with five possible entrances. The banks are low and of little use defensively, and it is likely that this was just such a seasonal camp for the people of the area. There is also evidence that beneath some of the later Iron Age hillforts, older structures once existed. Carl Wark, above the Derwent Valley, and Fin Cop in the Wye Valley are good example of hillforts constructed on top of much older and already ancient sites.

It was about this time that bank barrows appeared, huge, exaggerated long barrows, extending for hundreds of metres from a chamber at one end. Long Low above the Manifold Valley is the only example to be found in the area.

Slightly later came the henges, which were large circular enclosures usually surrounded by a deep ditch and outer bank. Within the henge would often have been a ring of large wooden posts sometimes surrounding a central pillar. In areas where good hard rock was readily available, these timbers circles were later replaced by rings of stones, and it was from this time that the first true stone circles, without the surrounding henge, began to be built. Again, the purpose of all these enclosures is a matter of conjecture, but it seems that some at least were aligned with the rising and setting of the Sun and the Moon on significant days of the year and it is very likely that religious ceremonies took place within them.

In the Peak District, the henge at the Bull Ring near Doveholes is the best example of an early henge, while that at Arbor Low retains not only an internal stone circle but also a central cove of larger stones. The only other circle in the Peak that possibly dates from the Neolithic period is the now much reduced Nine Stones Close below Robin Hood's Stride.

All of these early structures are associated with burial and ceremonial practices. Because of this it is difficult to discover any details of the day to day lives of these people. From what we do know it can be safely assumed that they lived in a structured and co-operative society. They certainly believed in an afterlife or at least a continuity of spirit, resulting in a continuing respect for the dead. Therefore, they must have had a religion of some sort, and certain places were of religious significance to them.

They had many skills and could make a wide variety of tools and implements from stone and bone and wood. Some of these tools, such as stone axes, were developed to such an art form that they became more than just utilitarian. Many examples have been found, beautifully polished, but unused and buried within or close to ceremonial sites.

We also know that they were made from stone found in only a few locations about the country. In the Peak District, examples of stone axes from all the major axe 'factories' of Britain have been found. From the distance that many of these axes had been brought, it must be assumed that the place where they were made was of importance and added to the symbolic power of the axe.

As well as stone they also carved bone, which was shaped into a wide variety of useful tools, and from the few fortunately preserved examples of woodwork we know they were skilled in this craft too. They could make baskets and fences, and over wet ground they constructed wooden walkways and bridges. They built canoes and rafts, which were capable of crossing not only rivers and lakes but also the open sea. They knew how to make pottery and fire it in simple kilns. They made round-bottomed pots that were both functional and decorative. In some of the chambered cairns, like Green Low, shards of such pottery were found broken alongside the bones of those interred.

We also know that they could quarry because they cut enormous blocks of stone from the hillsides and that they also had the technology to transport them over great distances. They could mine, and in eastern England they dug for flint in shafts over 30 feet below ground. In Lathkill Dale they quarried the local chert, which is found in narrow seams in the limestone, using antler picks to prise out the hard stones.

They had also started to change the landscape on a significant scale. Great swathes of the forests had by now been cleared to make way for crops and grazing, and the wild-woods had retreated into the wetter lowlands and the steeper slopes of the hills. They understood trade, and as farming methods developed it is likely that a degree of specialism and marketing of produce had begun.

Neolithic amulet

If we assume that the Sun and the Moon were important to them, were these their gods? On midsummer evening, someone standing within Nine Stones Close would have seen the full moon framed in the twin towers of Robin Hood's Stride away to the south. Did they still believe in these 'special places', the mountain tops, the springs and the caves which their forefathers had so revered? From the positioning of their circles and burial cairns so close to these ancient places it must be assumed that they did, and that although the method of worship developed and changed, the significance of certain special places still held good in the social memory of the people.

They began to use the caves once more. Caves which had been a source of shelter for their ancestors now began to be used as their tombs. Small caves and narrow fissures, often hidden away in secluded valleys or in inaccessible cliffs were chosen to be places where the dead were placed. There is evidence that ceremonies were often carried out within the caves, fires lit and offerings burnt, hidden away from all but those allowed to be present.

Carved idols have been found in stone and wood and bone, and many of these resemble the enlarged female form. This has led to the belief that they worshipped an 'earth mother' an embodiment of the natural forces and features which surrounded them.

Other forms of art are more of a mystery. Geometric patterns of circles and spirals, lozenges, zig-zags and hollows known as 'cup marks', have been found. These patterns are often found on the pottery placed, or sometimes deliberately broken, inside the places of burial. At some sites, these symbols have been painstakingly cut into the very stones of the barrows, while in other places they appear on single stones found on remote and isolated moors. On Eyam Moor, a portal stone to a ring cairn is dotted with deep circular cup marks, and on Gardom Edge cup marks within rings can be found

Neolithic 'Goddess'

carved into a low flat rock. What purpose did these carvings serve? Was it 'art' to be simply admired, or did it have a meaning that we no longer understand. Either way it does indicate that our Neolithic ancestors were a complex people whose thoughts and beliefs went far beyond simple superstition and were possibly as intricate as those that exist today.

Despite the obvious differences that would have existed in a land of such varied landscapes and climates, everything suggests that this was largely a homogenous and peaceful society. There is little evidence of warfare between tribes and little need for defensive structures, and it has been described as a 'golden age', when man was in harmony with the landscape and with his fellow man. In reality, however, it is more likely that as the Neolithic period drew to a close, the life of the common man in this undoubtedly complex and spiritual society was probably as short and harsh as at any other period of our history.

In all probability the Bronze Age arrived in Britain largely unnoticed by the majority of its inhabitants. It was just another innovation brought by traders or incomers from the south, the ability to use metal. Gold had been known for many years and had been fashioned into ornaments and jewellery, but it was the discovery of bronze, an alloy of copper and tin, which was the most significant leap forward.

It is quite likely that to the people of the time, other developments had a greater impact on their day to day lives. The weaving of wool to make warm and comfortable clothes and blankets was just one of the many important stepping-stones to civilisation that occurred in this period. The domestication of the horse would have begun to revolutionise travel, especially when combined with the concept of the wheel, the first known examples of which date from about this time. However, it was the coming of the ability to use metal which would kick-start the great social changes that would engulf the country over the next millennia.

Unlike gold, copper could be found quite easily in many areas and once it was discovered that it could be mixed with tin, to make a metal harder than either of them, a new industry and a new era dawned.

On a practical level it would have made little difference, although it now became possible to make very sharp and durable blades and tools, but probably of more significance was the mystique which would have surrounded the process. If the 'magic' that created the shiny metal was strong, so too was the 'magic' that the blades themselves possessed.

Just as some stone axes were symbolically potent, even more so would be these new objects of bronze. Their importance can be gauged by the number of them found buried with the dead or within circles and barrows.

In the same way, the people who possessed such powerful symbols would have held a status unthought of before. Copper could be found locally, it was certainly mined near Ecton in the south of the Peak from the early Bronze Age, but tin could only be obtained from Cornwall. Because of this, bronze would have remained a rare, and therefore, much-valued material. This rarity, combined with the skill required to forge the tools, would have greatly added to the 'power' of possessing them.

The homogenous society of the early Neolithic had already begun to break up, but now came a sudden rise in the number of people who seemed to have held a higher status in society than the common man. The era of the large communal burial site came to an end and from now on it seems that only certain individuals were buried within large and imposing cairns and tumuli.

Individual stone coffins or cists now held a single body, often accompanied by grave goods indicative of their wealth. Bronze axes and arrowheads, jewellery and ornaments were placed alongside the

bodies, and with them were
ceremonial beakers containing food and water to accompany the soul to the afterlife.
There is even some evidence
to suggest that flowers were
placed on the bodies, in a
custom that continues to the
present day. In other areas,
bodies were cremated and the
ashes placed within a pot
before a final burial.

These people have become
known as the Beaker People,
and it was long supposed that
they were an influx or 'inva-
sion' of people from the continent, who revolutionised the
way of life in Britain. More
likely, was that it was the ideas
which spread, possibly by new

Bronze Age 'beaker'

settlers, to the indigenous population who then adopted them.

As the way of life began to change, so too did the focus of their society. In the Peak District the area of the White Peak seams to have diminished in importance as it is on the higher plateaus of the East Moors and
the southern fringe of the Dark Peak that the next phase of monument
building took place. Almost all the small stone circles, ring cairns and
enclosures are to be found on these higher areas. In the Neolithic period
the circles were large and widely spaced, but with the coming of the
Bronze Age, there numbers increased dramatically, and their size
diminished. This possibly tells us that the large tribal groupings of the
earlier period were now breaking up into smaller communities and
family settlements.

In some places several circles were built close together. Perhaps
each served a different family group, or it could be that over time new
circles simply replaced the older ones. Some were true circles and other
elliptical, and some even had a large central stone. Some were built on
artificially levelled platforms and some were graduated with the tallest
stones placed opposite the smallest. Some were tiny and barely circles

Barbrook 111

at all, consisting of only four or five small stones, although this type is more commonly associated with Scotland and Ireland. On the Big Moor above Curbar Edge there are at least three circles still surviving and originally there were probably at least several more.

Quite why the geographical shift occurred at this time is not fully understood, but it is possible that the changing farming methods were now better suited to the higher gritstone lands. It is even possible that within the area of the Peak itself, different customs and beliefs were held in different districts.

It has been suggested that these monuments were originally wide-spread throughout the whole area, but were cleared off the lower lands by the enclosing of the fields in more recent times, but there is little evidence to support this. Certainly the construction of barrows continued across the whole of the area, but the tumuli which now covered these higher status burials were smaller and mostly round, hundreds of which still lie scattered across the whole area. They are found in a variety of forms and sizes, some built of earth and others of stone. Some had a ring of kerbstones around the base of the mound, while others had platforms built into them. On the East Moors, Hob Hurst's House is very unusual, being almost square in shape.

In some places whole cemeteries of these burial cairns were built.

On Stanton Moor there are the remains of over seventy cairns and tumuli. Many others were built on the summit of prominent hills or on the skyline where they could be seen for miles, in a practice that continued the trend begun thousands of years before with the great longbarrows. In some cases, such as Arbor Low, Bronze Age tumuli were actually added to already ancient Neolithic monuments, again confirming this idea of a continuity of the importance of some 'special places'.

Most individual standing stones also date from this era. Again their purpose is difficult to interpret. Many stand close to circles as outliers and may have been to mark the rising or setting of the Sun on significant days.

Others definitely marked the routes of the many ancient trackways which crossed the land. Surviving standing stones are rare in the Peak District, many having been broken up, while others have fallen and been lost amongst the heather. The ones at Warksworth and on Gardom Edge are examples of ones standing in isolation while the King's Stone is a small outlier to the Nine Ladies on Stanton Moor.

As the Bronze Age drew to a close, the break up of society into regional tribal groupings became more intense. Individuals of high status rose to power and rivalries between areas and tribes developed. This was fuelled by the problems of a rising population and an increasing competition for land. On Mam Tor we have one of the best examples of a late Bronze Age settlement in the country, illustrating the growing need for societies to have a focal point where people could gather for trade or security. Here a single bank and ditch with two inturned entrances enclose the large hill top, within which numerous platforms show where individual huts were sited. It would seem that the enclosure was developed and strengthened over time, spanning a period when the changing way of life resulted in an increasing need for places of safety.

For it was at about this time, around 1 000 BC that there was also a general deterioration in the weather. It became much colder and wetter and some upland areas became no longer viable for farming. This would have added to the growing pressure on the already crowded and deforested lowlands. The result of this would have been the need for communities to defend or take land to sustain themselves. This resulted for the first time in the construction of strongly defended sites and the significant production of weapons for more than just hunting.

This rise in aggression between tribal groups would have been made worse by yet another innovation which reached Britain by about 800 BC, the smelting of iron!

Easy to find and to extract, iron was very different from bronze. The 'power' of these new weapons came not just from the symbolic importance of their possession, but in their use. Powerful weapons lead to the rise of powerful individuals and groups. Warlords rose by strength and tribal boundaries were made and broken as the fortunes of war ebbed and flowed. Great forts were built on the hills, defended by huge banks and ditches. Their still-substantial remains are still scattered across the hilltops of the Peak. There is also a suggestion that the worsening weather lead to retreat from the hills, the population declining significantly with a migration into the surrounding lowlands.

For those that remained life would have became more difficult, agriculture more marginal, and the struggle for survival more consuming. For most people, burials were now largely unmarked. Perhaps as life became more brutal, death became less significant, and perhaps even the power of the old gods lessened as the power of the iron weapons increased.

What we do know is that the stone circles and henges were gradually abandoned and although they were still seen as special places, the people seem to have returned to their older beliefs. Once again it was the natural features of the landscape, the pools and springs, trees and caves that became the focus of their religion. A priesthood grew up and these 'Druids' surrounded themselves in a lore which to the common man must have seemed both magical and mystical.

These changes happened slowly as society continued to evolve and develop, largely from within, forced upon them by changing circumstances, although trade across the Channel and the Irish Sea ensured a gradual flow and exchange of ideas and innovations. So it would have continued, had it not been for the most cataclysmic event ever to occur in our long history. On one fateful day in the spring of 43BC the first of the vast legions of Rome set foot in Britain. With them they brought a culture which would sweep through England and supersede if not completely replace all that had existed before. They also brought with them the written word and by so doing, ended for ever the prehistory of our land.

So what, if anything, have our prehistoric ancestors left us? Is there anything beyond the few abandoned stones and mounds that lie scattered across our hills? The answer is yes, they have left us much more.

In fact their legacy to us is the very foundation stones on which our modern civilisation is built.

Some place names which sound so familiar to us, of our rivers and towns, our hills and vales have been passed down through thousands of years, and originated before our modern languages began. Many other words still in use today might well have been recognisable to the people who raised the great stones thousands of years ago.

Many of our older churches are built within and upon ancient stone circles or henges, while others stand beside natural springs and wells or where ancient trees once stood. At Bradbourne, the Anglo-Saxon church was built beside a much more ancient stone. The continuity of these special sites remains and many of us still worship in the same places as did our distant ancestors. The flower festivals and the custom of well dressing, unique to the Peak District, almost certainly date back for thousands of years.

Many of the religious ceremonies which the Christian faith still cele-brate throughout the year were 'borrowed' from the older faiths, and we still decorate Yule Logs, paint Easter eggs and kiss beneath the mistle-toe. The skull and crossed thigh-bones is still recognised as the symbol of death, and we still spread flowers on our graves. We live by a calen-dar still based on the cyclical movements of the Sun and the Moon, and are affected by their changing positions and phases. We continue, often unknowingly, traditions more ancient than we imagine.

Many of these old beliefs and customs still cling on, often as no more than superstitions, but every time we 'touch wood', cross our fingers or toss a coin into a pool we are reaching back into the past, touching a time and a place that we do not realise that we remember.

The ancient stones are a part of us and we a part of them. The ancient monuments of the Peak are not only a part of our heritage, but have an importance which is recognised World-wide. We have in our care some unique and intriguing prehistoric monuments and should be justly proud of them. We owe it to our children, and to our children's children to care for them and preserve them. We must respect them as a part of our history, a part of what makes us what we are, and remember that they are our window back into the time before History began.

The Dark Peak

Hordron Edge stone circle

1. Mam Tor
Castleton

Approx. distance: 6 miles

Approx. time: 4 hours

Starting point: Castleton GR 149830

Grade: A straightforward and very popular walk over high hills

O.S. Maps: Explorer sheet OL 1; Landranger sheet 110

Grid references: Mam Tor GR 127836; Lose Hill GR 153854

Tucked away at the head of the lovely Hope Valley, the pretty village of Castleton is one of the most popular tourist centres in the Peak District. To the north a high ridge of shapely hills form the near horizon, while to the south the edge of a limestone plateau is deeply notched with spectacular gorges. Dominating everything is Mam Tor, the sacred 'Mother Mountain', an eminence so important that even its name has been passed down to us from the very depths of prehistory.

On its high windswept top is an ancient settlement, encircled by huge defensive banks and ditches, while just below it is the pass of Windy Knoll, the high point of an important ancient trackway running from the western lowlands into the high valleys of the central Peak.

This walk begins in Castleton, itself a very old settlement. A Norman Castle overlooks it, its square keep perched precariously between steep limestone gorges. At its feet, the village is a tight maze of lanes and alleys surrounding a busy main street.

Near to the church the main street bends sharply and a quiet lane known as the Hollowford Road runs off to the north. It passes over the Odin Sitch, the stream which flows down from the head of the valley, and the old village burial ground to reach the Hollowford Centre. From there a track branches off to the right which leads to a footpath across fields to join another lane beside Losehill Hall, the study centre for the National park. After only a short distance along the lane another path turns off to the left following the line of a stream flowing down from the hills. This path climbs steadily uphill, passing between Fields Farm and Riding House Farm and out onto the open sheep pasture beyond. It

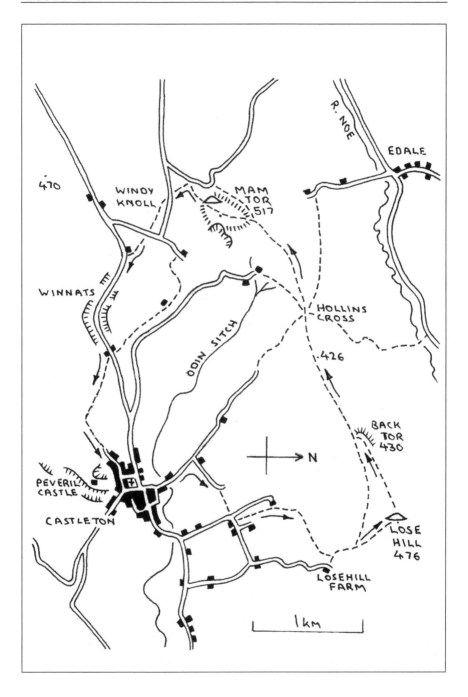

swings away to the right in the direction of Losehill Farm, but turns sharply uphill before it reaches it onto open 'access land'. There it joins a good, partly-paved track which climbs up onto the top of Lose Hill.

This rather complex approach is in reality quite straightforward, is well signposted and easy to follow. In springtime the streams are fringed with bluebells and pink campions, and tiny marbled lambs chase each other across the short-cropped turf. As the path rises the views widen, stretching away to the east towards the Derwent Valley, and to the west, where Mam Tor stands tall at the head of the valley. Only the incongruous tower of a distant cement works scars the scene, and even this is almost lost in the immensity of the wide landscape.

The summit of Lose Hill opens up a three hundred and sixty degree panorama. To the north the huge bulk of Kinder Scout rises above the beautiful Noe Valley, while to the east Stanage Edge can be clearly seen beyond the shapely ridge of Win Hill. Southwards the rolling hills of the White Peak fade into the distance and to the west a high, snaking ridge drops to Hollins Cross before rising again to Mam Tor. Even at this distance the ramparts of the great hillfort are clearly visible. The viewpoint on the summit actually sits on a Bronze Age tumulus although it is now barely recognisable as such.

Mam Tor from Back Tor

The ridge drops down from Lose Hill and a well paved and stepped track follows its crest to the next rise which is Back Tor. Its craggy top is another excellent viewpoint and a perfect place to stop and rest, and look across to the 'Mother Mountain' which is now looming closer.

The ridge dips then rises again before dropping down to the high col of Hollins Cross. As well as the ridge walk, at least six other paths meet here as they cross over the watershed between the two valleys. From there the ridge rises in a gentle curve, the paved pathway leading directly into the mouth of the great northern entrance of the hillfort.

Almost encircling the hilltop is a great defensive bank and outer ditch, only stopping where the natural cliffs fall steeply into the valley to the east. The fort dates from the late Bronze Age when the high bank was originally capped with a wooden palisade. This was later replaced with a 'revetted' stone rampart (meaning 'faced with a layer of stone') which would have stood up to twelve feet above the ditch with the steep hillside falling away below it.

The enclosed area within the defences covers about sixteen acres. Almost a hundred hut platforms have been discovered there on the sloping ground below the exposed hilltop. These can still be seen in some places, especially when the sun is low or there is a light dusting of snow to highlight where they have been cut back into the slope. If all these platforms held huts at the same time then it would indicate a size-able population living within the fort.

If so, this is unlike most of the other defensive sites in the peak which seem to be much smaller in scale and either the homes of only a small elite group or the temporary refuge for the many who lived down in the valleys. Supplying so many with fuel and food and water would have required a very organised society and most likely a subservient popula-tion living outside the high walls. Perhaps the defences were not only to provide security, but also to intimidate and dominate those who lived below. If Mam Tor really was a long term settlement for a large number of people, then the need for security must have been paramount, as the practical problems of living in such an inhospitable place must have been enormous.

Even in late spring I have experienced a pleasant, sunny walk chang-ing within a matter of moments into a battle against the elements. Storm clouds swept up from the west in minutes and ice-cold rain swept in fierce waves across the open hilltop, lancing down from a sky of almost biblical darkness. The wind howled and whined over the exposed

Mam Tor in the Bronze Age

slopes and nowhere could shelter be found. Only the desperate would choose to spend a winter up on these harsh and unforgiving slopes.

On the highpoint in the centre of the settlement is a Bronze Age tumulus and another lies just inside the second entrance which faces the south-west. These great tombs almost certainly predate the settlement and would suggest that the hilltop was already a place of some significance before the defences were raised. The discovery of several stone axes, possibly buried as part of a ritual also adds weight to the theory that this was a sacred place long before the first huts were built.

Even on quiet days, the top of Mam Tor can be a busy place, with many people standing unknowingly on the now cobble-stoned tumulus beneath their feet. Fortunately the main path crosses straight across the hillfort entering and leaving by the two ancient inturned entrances, and so it is still possible to complete a circuit of the great ramparts in relative solitude. Only then will shadows of its long past begin to re-emerge. From the faint dints in the slope above the bank will reappear the squat conical huts which once stood there, the smell of wood smoke hanging over the hilltop, and the great wooden palisade fence will rise once again on the high bank looking out over the valley below.

The path down passes the second of the tumuli, a hollow-centred grassy mound, and drops steeply down between the high banks of the southern entrance and down steps to the high winding lane which crosses over the ridge at this point.

From there, several return routes are possible. One way is to cut down across the hillside to join the path which passes the Blue John and Treak Cliff Caverns to reach the outskirts of Castleton. My preferred route is the path which crosses over Windy Knoll to reach the head of Winnat's Pass and down it to the Speedwell Cavern. This follows what would have been an important natural track between valleys, or from the valley up onto the high ground, that would have been used by both men and animals for thousands of years before the fort was built beside it.

Winnat's Pass is spectacular, and even the traffic funnelling through its narrow defile cannot take away from its soaring limestone ridges and turreted cliffs. Dark cave mouths peer out from broken crags and scree slopes clothe the lower slopes. A path runs down a pleasant grassy swathe beside the road all the way to the famous show cave, and from there another path can be taken, skirting around the hillside to reach the narrow winding back lanes of Castleton.

The magnificent scenery, and an abundance of show caves in the nearby hills, make this a very busy area on summer weekends. For those seeking the solitude of the hills or who would prefer to visit ancient places without the company of crowds of people, this is a walk that needs to be carefully timed. Out of season is best, but a good alternative is the quiet of early morning or the low slanting light of dusk. It is only at these times that Mam Tor throws off its tourist cloak and becomes once again that mystical and powerful place that once so dominated the prehistoric landscape of the Peak. Odin Sitch and Lose Hill are names which take us back to the dark, pagan times of Nordic dominance after the decline of the Roman Empire, but the name 'Mam' is quite probably almost as old as the great hill itself.

2. Hordron Edge Bamford

Approx. distance: 7 miles

Approx. time: 4 hours

Starting point: Bamford GR 208836

Grade: A wild and rugged walk across often-trackless moorland. This walk should be avoided in the spring to prevent disturbance to the many ground-nesting birds

O.S. Maps: Explorer sheet OL1; Landranger sheet 110

Grid references: Seven Stones of Hordron Edge GR 215868; Bamford Moor stone circle GR 221845

Beneath the popular rock-climbing 'mecca' of Stanage Edge, stretches the almost trackless expanse of Bamford Moor. Sweeping away below the crags, this wild and windswept moorland rises then drops again to Bamford Edge where it finally plunges down into the Derwent Valley. Hidden away among the gentle folds of the land, protected by deep cloughs and sodden bogs are two stone circles.

One, well-known and regularly visited, sits on a low ridge above the broken slopes of Hordron Edge. The other, about a mile and a half to the south, lies nameless and forgotten, elusive and rarely visited, in the midst of the bleak vastness of the open moor.

The walk begins in Bamford, starting from the centre of the village and following a steep track up and out of the village through woodland. It soon meets a lane climbing up from the valley towards the moorland. Turning right it is only a short way to where a footpath turns off left onto the slope rising up towards Bamford Edge. The path climbs steadily until an old quarry is reached. From there, the route branches off to the left following the high ground towards the first crags of the 'edge'. Once the crags are reached it is possible to follow a narrow path which weaves its way along the top of the broken cliffs.

To the right is the moor rising up to its domed top, where beneath the heather are a number of ancient burial cairns and tumuli. Down below is the Derwent Valley and the great dam holding back the huge Ladybower Reservoir. Beyond it, the great moorland fastnesses of

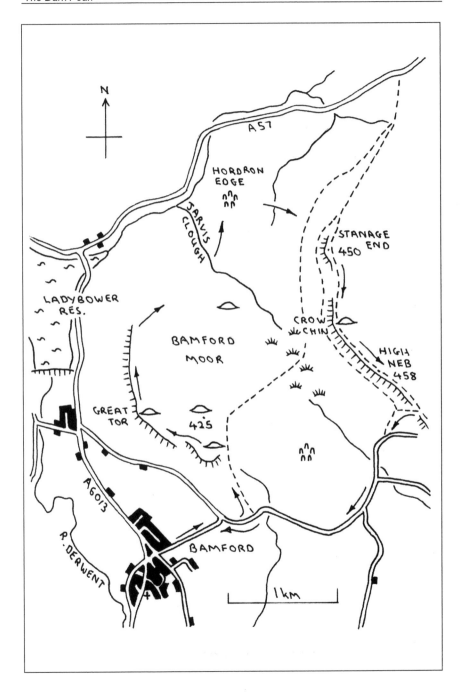

Kinder Scout and Bleaklow form the northern horizon. Off to the left and much nearer is the shapely top of Win Hill, a sacred summit in ancient times and almost certainly significant in the siting of the Hordron Edge circle from where it commands the skyline.

After about half a mile the craggy edge begins to peter out and starts to drop down towards the valley. It is at this point that our route turns away from the edge and crosses over the shoulder of the open moor. It is not easy walking, for the patchwork quilt of the moor is made up of thick heather interspersed with areas of reeds, tussock grass and sphagnum moss. Dry and sometimes burnt heather can in the matter of only a few feet become a deep, green morass of spongy moss and reed. Shallow cloughs drain the moor and even the slightest hollow will hold water through the driest of seasons. Keep where possible to the highest ground, and head north-east, passing through a line of old, abandoned, stone fence posts until the main feature of the moor is reached.

This is Jarvis Clough, a deep but shallow-sided valley. The stream which tumbles down it, rises in the wet heart of the moor below the steep cliffs of Crow Chin which can now be seen off to the right. In the clough is a small open shelter which is used predominantly by the grouse shooters but which can also be a welcome refuge for walkers when the weather turns.

From the shelter there is a good track which rises onto the moor beyond and follows the line of Hordron Edge towards the Sheffield Road about half a mile away.

Hordron Edge with Win Hill on the skyline

This track is followed until a picturesque stone circle comes into view off to the right, on the crest of the low ridge above the edge. These are the Seven Stones of Hordron Edge. In reality there are ten standing stones and the stumps and remnants of at least eleven others, in a circle about twenty paces across. The tallest stone is only between three and four feet tall and most are much smaller, but it is the location which makes it such an imposing place to visit.

Not far to the east are the impressive cliffs of Stanage Edge with the sheer buttresses of Stanage End and Crow Chin at either end. To the north-west, the moors rising towards Dovestone Tor are crowned with the strange rock formations of the Hurkling Stones and, to the south-west, are the conical summits of Win Hill and Lose Hill.

The tallest stone is known as the Witch's Stone and there are many tales of mysterious lights and strange happenings associated with the stones. Whether you believe in such things or not, it is certainly a very atmospheric place. When the stones were first raised, the surrounding ring of important natural features must have played some part in the decision to site them where they are. Today it is just a lovely spot to sit in, to soak up the atmosphere and enjoy the marvellous all-round panorama.

From the circle the route heads east, heading directly for the crags of Stanage End. There is no path and it is again best to stick wherever possible to the higher ground, skirting around the shallow but swampy clough which drains away to the north. Once past it, the land rises towards the cliffs, the ground becomes much firmer and drier, and rock-strewn grassland largely replaces the thicker vegetation of the lower moor. This is a wonderful area for birds. Meadow pipits, wheatears and skylarks are everywhere, lapwings and curlews call incessantly and red grouse skim noisily away over the heather.

As the slope steepens, a good track is crossed which runs along below the cliffs, but far better to scramble up between the rocks to find the path along the top of the 'edge'. This path is well trodden, used by the countless rock climbers who flock to these famous cliffs, but it is possible to pick your own route, hopping from rock to rock along the edge enjoying the spectacular natural architecture of the crags and the sweeping views below. The tiny circle of Hordron Edge can still be made out far below.

There are three, small, circular water-filled hollows on the highest rock of Stanage End which may well be man-made and ancient, unlike the many other basins which can be found all along the 'edge'. These shallow rock pools all have drainage channels carved out of the rock to feed them, and each is numbered. I can only assume they were cut at some time in the more recent past to provide water for grazing animals in the drier months.

The path dips, then rises past three ancient cairns to the trig point marking the top of High Neb. About a hundred metres past it, a good track cuts down through a wide gully to allow you to rejoin the lower path. It was in that gully that I saw a pair of ring ouzels moving along the cliff line making their nervous 'clicking' call to each other as I passed.

From the lower track, a good path drops down the slope to join a rough lane leading towards the large car park used by the many climbers and walkers heading for the crags. Directly ahead, the moor dips into a shallow valley then rises gradually towards the distant high point of the moor. It is in the midst of that vast featureless slope that the second of the moor's stone circles is located.

I have not included the circle in the walk, simply because I can find no acceptable way of advising readers how to reach it. It is surrounded by a wilderness of deep heather and bottomless bogs and is marked by nothing that will indicate its position. For those intrepid enough to branch off the track and strike out across these intervening 'badlands', the rewards are never the less great. The circle is tiny, barely eight paces

Bamford Moor stone circle

across, and formed of seven small uprights standing on the inside edge of a low stone bank. It sits on steeply sloping ground but has been dug into the slope to produce an almost level central space. The stones hardly raise their heads above the surrounding heather, but their great charm lies more in their isolated location and the simple challenge of finding them.

If you do attempt it, I can offer only the following advice: avoid the low ground, use the surrounding hills to help plot the circle's position and be prepared to stumble over it accidentally after giving up all hope of ever finding it using more conventional methods. What I can promise you is that, once there, you will have it all to yourself!

From the car park the lane is followed down, around the hillside, dropping down off the moor to rejoin the track running back down the long slope into Bamford.

This is not an easy walk, and those attempting it should be prepared for rough going. In bad weather navigation would be challenging to say the least, but it does give the opportunity to branch away from the well-trodden paths and sign-posted security that has become so much a feature of our favourite National Park. It will also allow you the chance to experience ancient sites in wonderfully wild and beautiful scenery.

3. Carl Wark
Hathersage

Approx. distance: 7 miles

Approx. time: 4-5 hours

Starting point: Hathersage GR 234817

Grade: a very scenic walk over rugged and rocky terrain

O.S. Maps: Explorer sheet OL 1; Landranger sheet 110

Grid references: Higger Tor GR 256820; Carl Wark hillfort GR 259814; cairn GR 252814

Burbage Moor rises bleak and wild above the western suburbs of Sheffield. This great expanse of featureless, heather moor comes to an end at Burbage Rocks where it plunges suddenly and dramatically over spectacular, turreted cliffs into the valley of Burbage Brook. On the far side of the stream, and isolated from the surrounding edges, stands a flat-topped and cliff-ringed tor known as Carl Wark.

This spectacular natural rock-table became a sacred place to the prehistoric inhabitants of the area who almost certainly used it as a site of seasonal gatherings. Many generations later, as a worsening climate and a growing population led to growing hostilities between tribes, its natural defences were added to. The result is one of the most remarkable and best-preserved Iron Age hillforts in the north of England.

To get there, our walk begins in Hathersage, that popular haunt of walkers and rock climbers, on the rising slopes above the Derwent Valley. Just off the main street is a narrow road leading down into Dale Bottom, and a short way along it, a tiny lane climbs up towards the old church of St. Michael. It is worth pausing on the journey to visit the churchyard, where the grave of Little John, Robin Hood's trusty lieutenant, an ancient yew and the stump of a medieval cross can all be found.

The route itself takes the track which turns off to the right just before the church is reached, and winds between the last of the cottages and out into the hills behind. It is followed to Carr Head House, where a path climbs up the steep hillside to rejoin the track much higher up. Turning right it is only a few hundred metres to reach the road.

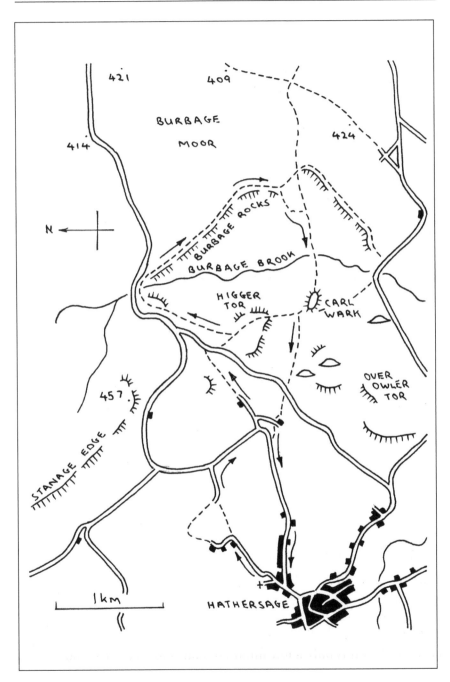

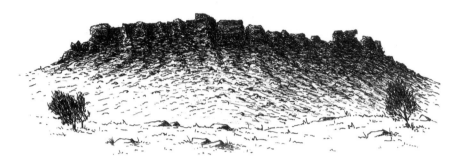

Carl Wark

This is the high moorland road which climbs up over the shoulder of Stanage Edge, before dropping down to Sheffield. Instead of turning up towards the high pass, our route follows the road downhill. The wetland to the left of the road is a haven for birds. I watched as flocks of small waders circled and landed in the shallow reedy pools, lapwings twisted and turned in the sky and a single curlew flew low and straight over the heather.

At the first sharp bend, we take a farm track turning off to the left, climbing up past the ruined farmhouse at Callow and on up the steep hillside behind. As it begins to level out, the turreted crags of Higger Tor appear over the near skyline. After crossing another moorland road, a wide path leads onto the Tor itself.

This spectacular, rocky plateau is worth exploring. Two broken edges converge to form a sharp prow of high ground standing up above the wide, shallow valley of Burbage Brook. Across the valley, the broken edge of Burbage Rocks form a sharply serrated skyline, while to the south, the strange pinnacles of Over Owler Tor stand up from their high ridge. In the centre of this huge, natural amphitheatre rises Carl Wark, the object of our walk. To reach it, our route is going to circle around the rim of the valley and approach it from the far side in order to savour the wildness and isolation of this ancient, sacred place.

After retracing our steps for a short way, another footpath is taken which branches off to the north-east, dropping down initially, before crossing the moor parallel to the road. It eventually rejoins the road at two old bridges where the tributaries of Burbage Brook tumble down from the upper moor into the valley. The path skirts around below the road, crossing both streams before turning away once more towards the broken edge of Burbage Rocks. A good track runs along below the edge but the smaller path along the top of the rocks gives far better views.

Keeping as close as possible to the edge, a path can be found which weaves alongside the shattered edge, where tottering towers and turrets of weathered gritstone lean over the crags below. Amongst the boulder field below, gnarled, hoary birches and stunted oaks shelter in the shadow of the rocks.

On my last visit, the clouds suddenly, and unexpectedly dropped, covering the high moorland and the view became reduced to little more than a stones throw in any direction. Spectral streamers of mist weaved between the outcrops and beads of moisture clung to every sprig of the heather. Towers of rock appeared briefly, only to be swallowed up again by the grey tide lapping against the cliffs. What is, on a sunny day, a pleasant stroll took on a wildness that stripped away all evidence of the modern world. It left instead only that which our ancestors would have seen as they too searched for the way down into the valley.

Then, as is the way with such weather, the clouds lifted, the edges shook off the last of the clinging mists and the way ahead became clear. The edge peters out into a shallow valley before rising again beyond it. A narrow path drops down to the lower track and then on down again to the where the stream emerges from a large plantation in the valley bottom. It is crossed by a lovely old, stone, packhorse bridge. Beyond the bridge, the land climbs again to where the crenulated ridge of Carl Wark now dominates the view, rising like a miniature 'Lost World' above the valley.

The path climbs steeply, heading directly for the natural, rocky ramparts of the fort. These are quite easily scrambled through to arrive inside the enclosure.

Covering an area of about two acres this raised table-land would have been an obvious and very conspicuous feature of the ancient landscape. There is a close similarity between this site and the better documented one on the crest of Gardom's Edge. Standing on an isolated but prominent edge, partially ringed with cliffs, and at a point where a number of ancient paths met, the site would have been unsuitable for habitation because of the jumble of huge 'earthfast' (firmly lodged) blocks which almost covers its top. More likely is that it was a seasonal gathering place for the Neolithic people of the area.

To add weight to this theory is a deep, water-filled rock basin which appears to have been carved into the top of the highest rock-tower which stands up above the cliff-edge on the north of the plateaux. If ever there was a place of ritual it was surely here on this natural pulpit!

What is certain is that Carl Wark was turned into a defended site in the later Iron Age, and was used as such up to and after the Roman conquest. To the north and east the natural rocky ramparts were sufficiently steep to require no extra defences, while the gentler edge to the south was capped with a wall of large blocks of stone set into the ground or added to the existing rocks. The gentlest slopes facing west were defended by a ten foot high earthen bank faced on its outside with a remarkably well-preserved wall of huge gritstone blocks. There is only one entrance, in the south-west corner, where the man-made walls turn inwards, allowing a natural rocky ramp to rise into the centre of the fort.

Because of the huge wind-sculptured rocks which litter the top, it was unlikely to have been used as a place of long-term residence, serving instead as a place of refuge in times of trouble for the local people. They would probably have lived below the fort to the south where the traces of ancient field systems and a number of cairns can still be found.

It is an impressive view point, the land sloping away in all directions before rising again to sharp edges which almost ring the skyline. Only to the south is the ring broken, where the brook drops down through the aptly named 'Toad's Mouth', into the valley of the River Derwent. Dominating everything is Higger Tor just a short distance to the north. With

Inturned entrance to Carl Wark

its soaring buttresses and tottering pinnacles it also looks more like a fortress than a natural outcrop.

The return route takes the path towards the Tor for a short distance before branching off to the left, passing below its crags in the direction of a small copse of rowan trees on a shallow col. Just above the trees, on the top of a low, rounded hill are the remains of one of the many ancient burial cairns of the area.

From the col the path drops down, over a lane, and on down to the isolated house of Mitchell's Field. After skirting around the house, the route drops into a steep-sided, narrow valley and up its far bank to reach the road. This is then followed pleasantly down, through Dale Bottom, to arrive back in Hathersage.

This route offers just one of a huge variety of walks which can be used to explore this fascinating valley. It is all Access Land, and for those with time it is worth exploring further. Carl Wark is, and was, the focal point of the area, but almost everywhere on the surrounding moors and edges are the fingerprints of our ancient ancestors.

4. Eyam Moor
Eyam

Approx. distance: 6 miles

Approx. time: 3-4 hours

Starting point: Eyam GR 216768

Grade: A short but difficult walk, with sections across a wild and trackless heather moorland

O.S. Maps: Explorer sheet OL 24; Landranger sheet 119

Grid references: Stanage ring cairn GR 215787; rock basin GR 218784; Wet Withens stone circle GR 225791; Eyam barrow GR 225792

The village of Eyam sits comfortably on a wide limestone shelf below the much higher and bleaker gritstone moors stretching away to the north. Its fascinating, yet harrowing history of the plague is what brings visitors in their hundreds to explore its streets and to imagine the unthinkable scenes which must have unfolded behind the mellow facades of its tiny stone cottages.

Yet Eyam is far older than the 17th century, far older than any of the structures that now survive within this old village. Only up on the moors above it are there still clues to its much more ancient past, and it is the search for these that is the main purpose of this walk.

It begins in the village itself, leaving it along a lane climbing up towards Eyam Bank, a steep escarpment which is one of the great physical divides of the Peak District. To the south is the White Peak, the great limestone plateau stretching away towards the valley of the Trent. To the north, above the Bank, are the moorlands of the Dark Peak, their high edges rising like great waves one beyond the other.

At the first sharp bend, a track turns off to the left and climbs steeply up to join another lane running along the top of the slope. Behind stretches the White Peak in all its glory, the nearby Middleton Dale dropping down into the deeper valley of the River Derwent. Beyond that, the hills roll away into the distance, the tree-capped top of Minninglow clear on the far horizon. The lane is followed to the left along the edge until it turns uphill again and climbs over a low crest. This opens up the view ahead, this time over the Dark Peak to the north.

From this top lane a track turns off to the right towards a triangle of

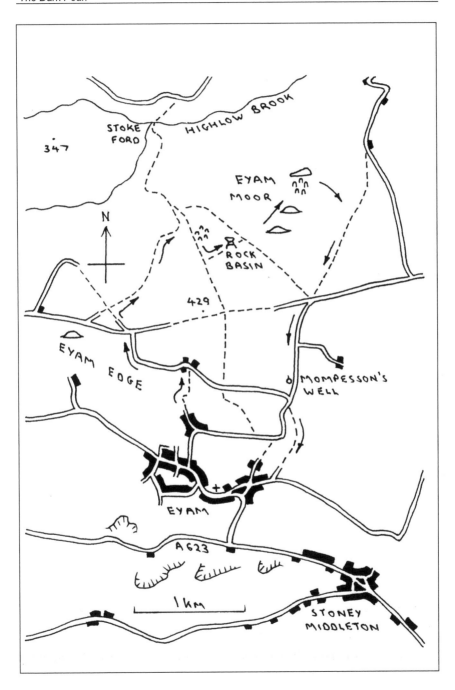

woodland, then right again towards Stoke Ford. It then runs through a strange but pretty area of huge rhododendron thickets, becoming a grassy path between tall beeches. It crosses several stone stiles to reach the edge of the moorland proper. The path continues on, skirting around the edge of the woodland, but our route takes a faint path climbing up onto the moors. After about a hundred metres it joins a much clearer path which is leading towards the high point of the moor. Beside this path, partly concealed in the heather, is Stanage ring cairn.

It is a circular bank of stones about fourteen paces across, surrounding an open space into which cremation burials would probably have been inserted. There is an obvious entrance facing north and marking one side of it is the only remaining large stone in the barrow. It is this portal stone which marks out this ring cairn from the many others scattered over the hills, because it is decorated with at least twenty-six deep cup marks.

These circular hollows cover the top and two sides of the stone which would suggest that it was originally built into the bank of the cairn with only these three faces showing. What the purpose of the cup marks was is still a mystery, perhaps a new one was carved each time a visit was made, or a relative was mourned. Perhaps they carried a message that we can no longer read, but they must have involved considerable time and effort. I wonder if they realised that their carvings would still be puzzled over thousands of years later.

From the ring cairn the path can be followed up the steepening slope until it levels out on a high shoulder leading up to the trig point. Off to the left of the track is a jumble of huge natural blocks of gritstone, and a

Cup-marked stone at Stanage Barrow

narrow path can be followed down to them. On the gently sloping top of one of these great earthfasts, there is a perfectly made circular basin holding a deep pool of black water, which acts like a mirror, reflecting the sky. Whether this is a truly ancient carving, linked with the nearby cup marks, or a more recent sculpture I don't know, but it certainly adds a sense of mystery to this wild place.

The path continues downhill for just a short way to reach a high stone wall which runs right across the moor, and this is followed to the right for about a hundred metres to where a narrow stile allows you to pass through to the lower moor.

This is a large trackless expanse of heather and reed, with bracken and bilberries encroaching on the lower slopes. In places the heather is deep and walking difficult, in others it thins and grasses and outcrops of rock break through to the surface. Through it all, a network of sheep tracks weave drunkenly, leading you tantalisingly in the right direction for short sections before veering off for reasons known only to the permanent residents of the moor.

The best advice is to keep to the left edge of the high ground as it curves away to the north. After a while the ground drops steeply away, and on the level moor below it should be possible to see the stones of Eyam barrow standing clear of the vegetation. As you approach it you will almost certainly stumble upon the stone circle which is hidden beneath the heather until you are almost upon it. Eleven stones remain, standing low on the inside rim of a low bank, which in places is higher than the stones. Only one stands clear, a strange, solid altar-like stone nearest the barrow and very different from the other low slabs. In the centre of the ring, which is over thirty paces across, is a shallow pit, which is possibly the remains of a later cist burial.

The barrow lies only thirty paces beyond the circle and almost certainly predates it. It is a long barrow, over thirty paces long and barely fifteen wide, and although now hollowed out it remains a substantial feature in the landscape. The two monuments are undoubtedly linked although one is older than the other. Together they make a fascinating complex, hidden away as they are, surrounded by views which are the equal of any in the area. Their remoteness greatly enhances the pleasure of finding them, and it is possible to sit there and experience a peace and tranquillity quite unusual in England today. It is interesting to think that this wild and desolate place is probably less visited now than at any time in the last five thousand years.

Because it is so quiet it has become a haven for wild life. Red grouse

Wet Withens and Eyam Barrow

are abundant, their cackling cries a constant interruption to the peace of the moor. Meadow pipits are everywhere and even the rare twite can be seen flitting shyly through the thick heather. Hen harriers, once almost lost as a breeding bird in England, have now returned and can often be seen hunting low over the slopes of Eyam Moor. And even though the heather covers most of the moor, an abundance of wild flowers flourish where the sheep graze.

The stones of the barrow provide a wonderful place to rest and look out over the moor, to watch the vast skyscape gradually changing and the great cloud shadows creeping slowly across the hillsides. I have never been to Eyam Barrow and seen another human being!

From the stones there are as many ways of returning as there are sheep tracks winding away into the heather. Probably the easiest and best is to head due east until after about five hundred metres a good path is reached. This climbs back up and around the higher slopes of the moor, offering excellent views away to the left towards Froggatt Edge before levelling out just before it meets a high lane.

This lane heads back towards Eyam, rising gently at first before dropping down towards the village. It passes Mompesson's Well, the site of a natural spring made famous as the place where the plague victims of Eyam left money in return for food in the 17th century. On a sharp bend, a path turns off to the left and drops quickly down through a wooded dell to join a lane on the outskirts of the Eyam. An interesting end to the walk can then be enjoyed, as you wander through the streets, discovering the more recent history of this very ancient place.

East Moors

Lost stone on Harthill Moor

5. The Big Moor Curbar

Approx. distance: 9 miles

Approx. time: 4-5 hours

Starting point: Curbar GR 245745

Grade: A long walk on good paths, over high and exposed moorland

O.S. Maps: Explorer sheet OL 24; Landranger sheet 119

Grid references: Stoke Flat stone circle GR 249768; rock shelter GR 265784; Hurkling Stone GR 269777; Swine Sty enclosure GR 269752; Swine Sty GR 270751

A bove the villages of Baslow, Curbar and Froggatt on the eastern slopes of the Derwent Valley, runs a high gritstone edge. The towers, pinnacles and slabs of these high broken crags form a spectacular and serrated skyline. Behind them, hidden from the valley, is a vast tract of moorland dropping gradually away to the east, known as the Big Moor. For thousands of years a community lived and farmed there, growing and declining, changing and adapting, until finally the climate worsened and the people retreated into the valleys.

The land probably looked then much as it does now, heathland broken up by patches of scrub and thin scattered woodland. Only then the soil would have been light and sandy, easily worked and containing enough goodness for the farmers to grow crops and raise livestock. Today the soil is acidic, peat blankets much of the ground and only a few sheep now graze the heathery heaths.

Because the moor has become so inhospitable it has remained relatively untouched over the intervening millennia, and many clues still remain to tell us about the lives of these people. Beneath the peat, ancient field systems can still be traced, and above it a rich variety of cairns, enclosures and stone circles can still be found.

To search for them, our walk begins in Curbar, a village of fine stone houses climbing from the banks of the River Derwent up the steep, rocky slopes of the valley towards Curbar Edge. It is best to park near the river by the old bridge, which has now been bypassed by the new main road.

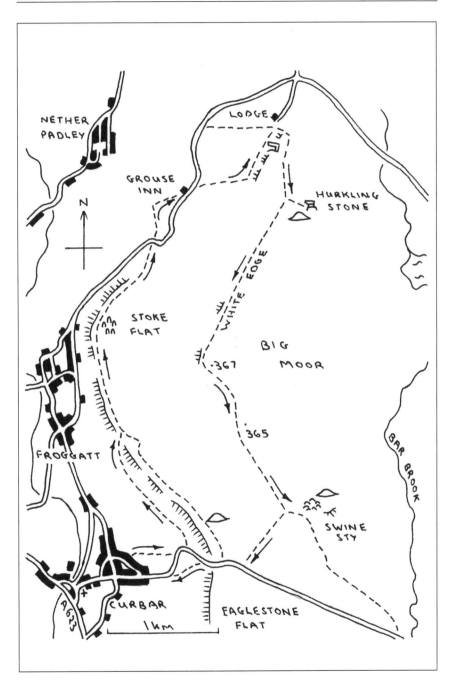

Curbar Lane climbs steeply up towards the main part of the village and this is followed until Pinfold Lane turns off to the left. This soon arrives at the village well, and another lane known as The Green continues past it. After about a hundred metres a footpath turns off to the left, passing through a playground and on through boulder-strewn fields to reach a lane. This is followed uphill for just a short way to a sharp bend, where a footpath branches off to the left and climbs up towards the looming crags.

This path meanders below the cliffs, giving endless opportunities to watch the rock climbers attempting the many climbs above. It weaves around huge boulders and scattered birch trees until it picks its way carefully between the crags and up onto the moors above the edge.

Here it joins the popular path along the top as it follows the broken crest of the crags northwards. Buttresses and pinnacles, towers and turrets rise up, wind-smoothed and weathered, as a fantastic foreground to the more distant views away over Eyam Moor and beyond.

The path drops gently down as Curbar Edge becomes Froggatt Edge, and as the scattered trees thicken, a small stone circle appears just to the right of the path. This is Stoke Flat. A wide stone bank forms a ring about sixteen paces across, from which several larger upright stones stand. The tallest, a much weathered pillar, is only 3-4 feet tall and stands beside one of the two possible entrances. It is a typical Bronze

Stoke Flat stone circle

Age circle, much smaller than the older circles of the White Peak, and was probably a ceremonial site for a small community living nearby. Whether the bank and circle are contemporary or one predated the other is not clear.

From the circle the path continues, dropping slowly down to where the main road climbs up onto the edge of the moors. On the far side of the road is another path, which drops down into a shallow wooded valley and passes through a car park, before crossing fields to rejoin the road beside the Grouse Inn.

Over the road another path is taken which climbs up through patchy woodland to a broken edge where the path forks. The left-hand route is taken, following below the edge towards the unusual White Edge Lodge. Just before it is reached, a small rock shelter appears in the rocky slopes above. At first sight, the huge slab which leans against the main crags appears to be covered with a spectacular array of cup marks. On closer inspection, however, many of the surrounding rocks also have many strange hollows and it is possible that they are a natural feature of the geology. Despite this, those on the slab itself do bear an uncanny resemblance to the man-made carvings found elsewhere in the area.

Just before the Lodge is reached, another path branches off to the right, climbing up to the top of the bank before turning back to the south. For the next three miles it follows the rising crest of White Edge. To the left of the path stretches the bleak expanse of The Big Moor, a wilderness of heather and reed and bracken with only the occasional stunted birch tree to relieve the flatness. It is a haven for wildlife and is a protected area. On my many crossings I have seen red grouse, short-eared owls and once a flock of golden plovers flitting nervously away from my intrusion. It is probably wilder now than in the Bronze Age, and if you can cross it early or late in the day, it is one of the few places in the Peak District where true solitude can still be found.

Off to the left of the path along the line of the only wall to cross it, is the strangely named Hurkling Stone, meaning 'the stone by the bilberries'. This large, tilted slab of natural rock is carved with old but not ancient symbols and provides the turning point of the wall and the district boundary and must once have been of some significance. Only a hundred metres away to the south-west of it are the remains of an ancient cairn, now almost lost in the heather. Further on is another old stone, which marked a crossroad of tracks which have now entirely vanished.

Rock shelter on White Edge Moor

The path climbs gradually up, following the steepening bank of White Edge until it reaches the highpoint marked by a trig point on a grassy knoll. From there it drops down to where the edge merges into the moorland sloping down towards the valley of the Bar Brook. The path then forks, the right-hand track leading back towards Curbar.

Before this is taken it is worth branching off the path and wandering over the moor in the direction of an area of broken crags to the left of the path, known as The Swine Sty. Between it and the path can be found a low circular enclosure about twenty paces across, similar in many ways to the circle at Stoke Flat with the exception that it has no upright stones. In parts the bank has almost merged into the landscape, but in others it can still be easily made out, with an inner ring of kerbstones forming a clear delineation between it and the central open space. Again it is small in scale, built to serve the small local community.

Just beyond it are several small clearance cairns, where surface stones have been cleared off the land for farming. The rocks of The Swine Sty itself are also worth exploring as there is evidence of ancient walls and small enclosures within them. Fortunately, this area has been intensely studied and has yielded up many details about the landscape as it must have been back in the early Bronze Age.

Largely buried now beneath the peat are the remains of many scattered smallholdings, each with garden plots and small fields possibly separated by hedgerows. Crops were certainly grown and domestic animals kept on land cleared from the surrounding scrub, lines of clearance cairns often marking the edges of cultivation. Buildings were probably quite simple and would be moved or replaced by successive generations, as new land was brought into use and old land rested.

Just beyond the road, on Eaglestone Flat, close to the prominent Eaglestone Tor, a small Bronze Age cemetery was found which contained the cremated remains of at least fifteen women and children. Some were interred in beakers and others were simply a scattering of ashes. Some graves were unmarked and others had simple stone settings, suggesting that it was used over a period of time. Were these people from the Big Moor? Why were the men buried elsewhere? Was the nearby 'tor' significant in the siting of the cemetery? As usual the evidence involves more questions than answers.

It is in fact, difficult to paint a clear picture of the Big Moor at any one particular time, as, like now, the landscape and the society that adapted it, would have been constantly evolving and changing. But what does seem certain is that this area of the East Moors was the home to a small population which lived and farmed there for at least two thousand years. It is fascinating to explore this ancient landscape, and from the few remaining clues, to try to recreate the 'lost world' of the Big Moor.

From The Swine Sty the route returns to the path which is followed down to the car park and the road, Eaglestone Tor clearly visible on the 'flats' beyond. The road then drops back over the edge, where a footpath cuts off the long bend, and then returns to the village.

6. Barbrook
Millthorpe

Approx. distance: 6 miles

Approx. time: 3-4 hours

Starting point: Shillito Woods Car Park GR 295750

Grade: A mostly straightforward walk on very good tracks, but Barbrook 11 can be tricky to locate

O.S. Maps: Explorer sheet OL 24; Landranger sheet 119

Grid references: Barbrook 1 GR 278756; reconstructed cairn GR 279757; Barbrook 11 GR 277758; Barbrook 111 GR 283774

B etween the wild and desolate stretches of Big Moor and Ramsley Moor, the Bar Brook flows southwards in a shallow valley to where it plunges steeply down to join the River Derwent. On the gently sloping land above the brook, but below the high moor, was a great necropolis of ancient burial cairns and a number of stone circles. Partly reconstructed, the site is an amazing place to visit, where monuments can be seen as they once were, yet set in a landscape still wild and beautiful.

Unlike the other walks in this book, this one doesn't start in a village, as this would necessitate several tedious miles along roads to reach it. Instead, it begins at the large car park at Shillito Woods, about two miles west of the small village of Millthorpe.

Close to the car park are two medieval crosses, one a short way along the lane to the north, and the other along a path into the woods. These can be easily visited prior to beginning the walk itself.

A well-marked path leads down from the car park onto the edge of Ramsley Moor, to join a good track which leads back to the lane a short distance further on. The lane is then taken westwards across the moor to Ramsley Reservoir. This is now little more than a small reedy pool hidden away behind the massive earth ramparts of the old dam. It is a haven for wildlife, and for those with a little time and a pair of binoculars, it is possible to see a wide variety of moorland and wetland birds. In fact the whole of Ramsley Moor behind has been designated as a wildlife sanctuary, and although now open Access Land it is requested that special care is taken not to disturb the birdlife, especially in the nesting season.

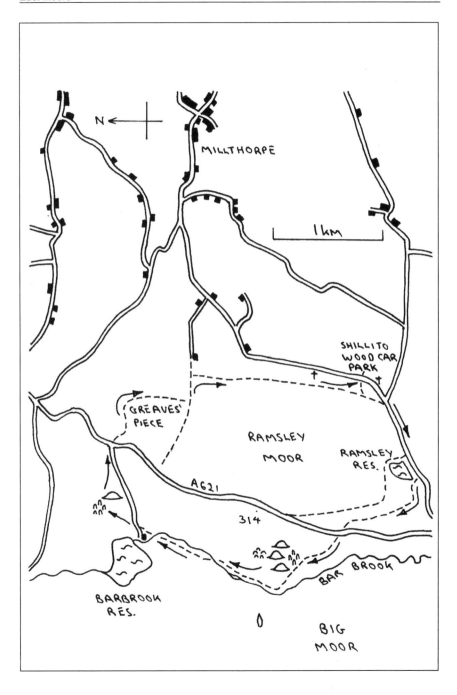

Barbrook 1 and restored cairn

From just beyond the reservoir, a path leaves the lane and climbs up over the shoulder of the moor to meet the main A621. The track continues over the road and on, across lovely sheep-cropped turf into the shallow valley of the Bar Brook. Beyond the valley the huge expanse of the Big Moor stretches away to the west, again an important sanctuary for the unique birdlife of the area.

Just a short way along the track is the first of the wonderful stone circles of the moor. This is Barbrook 1 and can be clearly seen from the track, just a short way off to the right.

About thirteen stones remain in a small circle about sixteen paces across. Some of the stones are barely more than low kerb stones around the inside edge of the stony bank which surrounds it, while others are slightly taller, rising to about three feet. The tallest stone has a large cup mark carved into one of its sides, and the next stone to it has several on its upper face. Within the circle the ground is quite level and was probably a prepared platform around which the stones were raised.

From the circle it is possible to see several burial cairns close by. The nearest is a partially restored cairn about fifty metres away to the north-east. This circular cairn is surrounded by a low drystone wall in place of the more usual kerb, and has a low additional platform added to it on its eastern side. Cremation burials were found within both the main cairn and the platform. Several of the larger cairn stones also had cup and rings carved into them. Another nearby cairn with what looks like the remains of a central chamber, seems to have a small leaning stone midway between it and the stone circle.

In fact, there are at least sixty cairns in the near proximity, hidden away in the folds of the moor. Many are now no more than low rocky hummocks partly lost beneath the heather and reeds, but others retain much of their original shape and size. Most are circular, some less obviously so, and some have larger kerb stones around them. Buried beneath one of the cairns was a polished stone axe, which was found to have come from the Langdale Pikes in the Lake District.

About three hundred metres away across the moor to the north is another circle. This is Barbrook 11, and is notoriously difficult to locate in the natural folds and creases of the moorland. It is a ringcairn, as opposed to a stone circle, although the differences seem to be only a variation on a theme. It has a central open space, roughly sixteen paces across just like Barbrook 1. It is surrounded by a revetted stone bank, on the inside rim of which are a number of upright stones. What is different is that the uprights are within, and mostly lower than a drystone wall which holds back the stone bank. It also has a marked entrance facing north-east, and the remains of a central cairn. Barbrook 11 has been restored, although to what extent and what accuracy I am not sure. Perhaps originally the two circles were quite similar.

What is clear is that these were places of ritual close to and almost certainly linked with the surrounding burial mounds, and the ancient settlement sites just a short distance away on the Big Moor.

It is a wild place nowadays, almost certainly wilder than it was in ancient times. Now there is little but the cry of the grouse and the song of the skylark to disturb the silence. The empty moor stretches away in all directions. Visited now by more sheep than humans, it is a delight to sit within its stones and wonder at the events which might have unfolded there thousands of years ago.

As I was doing just that, I noticed a stone within the encircling bank that looked different. I lifted it out and turned it over and found that I was holding a broken quern stone! One side had a perfectly smooth and slightly hollowed surface where it had been used as a grinding stone to produce the course flour, which was a staple food of the Bronze Age people.

I sat holding the stone and couldn't help but try to picture the face of the woman who had last used it. Was she young or old, happy or sad?

Was she in a cosy hut surrounded by her family, or alone on the edge of a bleak and windswept heath?

I also wondered how the quern had come to be in the ringcairn. Had it been broken accidentally and the useless pieces thrown carelessly onto the pile, or had it been broken ceremonially and the pieces presented as an offering to the

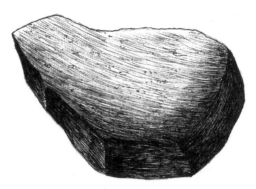

Quernstone from Barbrook 11

spirits? Was it to appease an angry god, to bring a fruitful harvest or to save an ailing child? There are many known examples of broken pots and axes being built into ritual sites. There are no answers, but the questions summon up images of the past that might have been, and bring a certain humanity to the dry stones of the old cairn.

I put the quern carefully in my rucksack and walked away, back towards the track beside the stream. Then I stopped, and turned back. Something told me to put the stone back where I had found it, so I did. I expect it's still there now. If you find it, look at it, let it paint its pictures in your mind, but then leave it for the spirits.

After returning to the track, it is followed gradually uphill as it rises onto the open moor past a small dammed pool on which geese can often be seen, to reach the larger Barbrook Reservoir. The track passes an isolated cottage and then swings away to the right towards the road. Up ahead, on the top of the low broad hill above the reservoir is the third of the Barbrook circles, Barbrook 111.

This is one of the largest circles in the Peak District, but is formed from the smallest stones. It is oval in shape, about twenty-six by thirty paces in size and is made up of about twenty tiny stones, which barely raise themselves above the level of the moorland grasses. Inside is a very flat platform free of all stones. There appears to be no surrounding bank, no interior cairns and all the circle stones lean markedly inwards towards the centre of the circle, resulting in a monument rather different from the others which are dotted about these moors. Perhaps it predated the others, although there are the remains of one circular, presumably Bronze Age cairn close by.

It sits now on a bleak and exposed heath, only the undulating call of the lapwings softening the whine of the wind, and unlike most stone circles always seems a rather uninviting place to sit and rest.

From there it is only a short way back to the track, which passes a tall stone waymarker pointing to Sheffield, before returning to the main road. Once across, the route continues down into Greaves's Piece, a rough heathland of bracken and reed dotted with rowan and hawthorn trees. It soon reaches a good track, which is followed downhill for a short way through woodland to where a bridleway turns off to the right. This pleasant path winds through the woods, over a stream and then climbs gradually up onto the more open expanse of Ramsley Moor to arrive back at Shillito Woods and the end of a fascinating and very worthwhile walk.

7. Gardom's Edge
Baslow

Approx. distance: 6 miles

Approx. time: 3 hours for the walk, but allow at least an hour to explore the edge.

Starting point: Baslow GR 256725

Grade: A magnificent walk on good paths, but with some steep slopes.

O.S. Maps: Explorer sheet OL 24; Landranger sheet 119

Grid references: The Eaglestone GR 263738; standing stone GR 273732; centre of enclosure GR 272729; carved stone GR 273730

Gardom's Edge stands high above the Derwent Valley, its steep, broken crags rising out of the dense oak and birch woodland which cloak its lower slopes. Separated from the other edges of the East Moors by the deep-cut side valleys of the Bar Brook and Umberley Brook, it stands like a great rocky prow above the town of Baslow. On the gentle slopes behind the crags are to be found the remains of a huge, Neolithic enclosure, and a treasure trove of other ancient monuments, which make it one of the most important and fascinating sites in the country.

To reach it our walk begins in Baslow, one of a line of small towns that climb from the banks of the River Derwent up the lower slopes of the valley. In the centre of the town, away from the main road, is a small triangular green, and from it a lane runs directly up the hillside behind. At the end of the houses it becomes a good track which climbs alongside a beech wood before breaking out onto open fields. Lined with hawthorn, elder and huge gorse bushes, it rises steadily towards the broken, craggy end of Baslow Edge. Away to the right the long line of Gardom's Edge can be clearly seen above the trees. The track narrows to a pack-horse trail, still cobbled in places, and weaves through an old quarried area to reach the top of the edge.

This is Eaglestone Flat, named after the Eaglestone, which is the enormous gritstone tor, about a hundred metres off to the left of the track. Over twenty feet high, this huge wind-sculptured block stands in isolation on the mostly featureless moor. Close beside it a Bronze Age

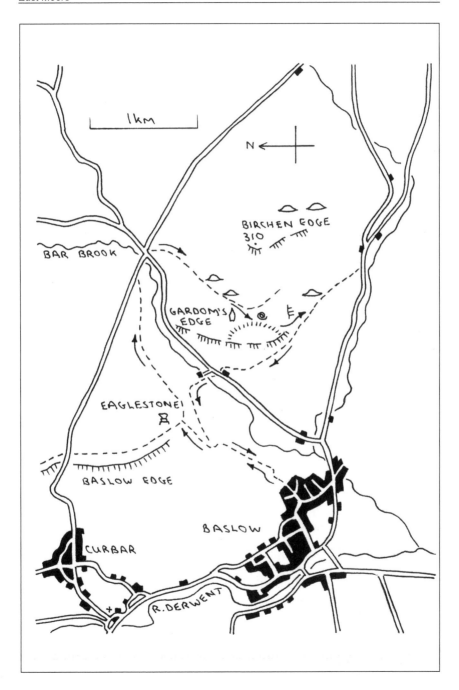

burial site was found where at least fifteen women and children were interred.

Our route follows the track eastwards, past the memorial cross to the Duke of Wellington, and along the top of the steep wooded slopes dropping away into the Bar Brook Valley. As the track drops, the moorland changes to high walled fields of pasture where wild-looking Highland cattle graze, before reaching a lane close to its junction with the main road crossing the moors. Cross over the road and through the gate leading onto the moors to the right.

Stretching before you now is Gardom's Edge, from the cliff edge to your right to where Birchen Edge rises up to the left in another tier of steep cliffs. Now that this is all 'Access Land' you are free to seek out its hidden treasures at your leisure. It is best initially to follow the good track which runs directly ahead into the centre of the heath. It is pleasant walking, over rough grass with patches of reeds and heather and a scattering of birch trees.

Before long it becomes obvious that beneath the vegetation there are banks and ditches everywhere, and small cairns where stones have been cleared from the land. To the left of the path a line of larger cairns and a wide stone bank run along a low ridge of higher ground. Many of these features date back to the Bronze Age when this land, like much of the high East Moors, was farmed. A small hut dating from this period has also been discovered here, and beneath its floor was buried the cremated remains of a young woman.

The highpoint of the edge lies in the area of thicker woods to the right of the main path and it is best to leave the path and head directly up the gently rising ground. Once into the trees it should be possible to see a large standing stone in a small grassy clearing ahead.

This strangely shaped, almost triangular blade of gritstone stands at least eight feet high. It is well weathered, with deep erosion grooves cut into its top and sloping sides. It leans as if to point up the slope towards where the great enclosure lies on the top of the hill. Perhaps it was indeed a marker or portal stone on the approach to the ancient site. As one of only a very few standing stones to survive in this area its rarity makes it all the more impressive.

Just beyond it, a matter of perhaps a hundred metres further into the sparse woodland, is the wide stony bank of the enclosure. This bank runs for almost six hundred metres in a gentle curve to meet the vertical cliffs of the edge at either end to enclose the highpoint of the edge. It can

Standing stone on Gardom's Edge

be followed for almost its entire length, only a short section at its southern end having been ploughed away in an encroaching field.

In places it can barely be made out amongst the natural bumps and hollows of the moor. In other parts it remains a high, wide bank of large blocks of stone built onto and over the natural scatter of earthfast blocks which litter the surface. In parts, longer stones have been placed vertically to form an outer façade. A number of entrances can still be identified, and it soon becomes obvious that it was not intended as a fortified site, despite the line of cliffs forming its western edge.

As well as the bank itself it is well worth exploring the cliff edge. Spectacular towers and turrets rise up above the level of the moor, and broad flat tables of rock jut out over the steep crags below. The wind and rain of millennia has carved the rock into fantastic shapes, and deep solution hollows hold dark pools of water reflecting the sky. In one part, just back from the edge, is a shallow, but sheltered dell where wizened old oaks grow from the exposed rocks. In several places the cliffs relent and gently sloping gullies offer possible routes of access from the valley below. Between the edge and the stone bank the ground is almost covered with broad flat earthfast boulders, making it extremely unlikely that it was ever a place of permanent settlement.

From the edge the view reaches far and wide, the Eaglestone and Curbar Edge to the north, and almost the whole of the White Peak stretching away to the west. As most other Neolithic monuments in the area are down on the lower hills of the limestone, it is significant that such an important place of meeting should be in such a prominent and visible site.

Unlike the great defensive hillforts of the Iron Age, or the ringed settlements sites of the Bronze Age, this enclosure seems to have more in common with the Neolithic causewayed enclosures more often associ-

Carved stone on Gardom's Edge

ated with southern England. Its many entrances and prominent isolated position would make it likely that this is in fact a very ancient meeting place where people from a wide area would meet for trade, festivals or religious ceremonies at certain times of the year.

Just outside the bank on the eastern side, and about halfway along its length is yet another amazing site. In a small grassy clearing, surrounded by a loose scattering of birch trees, is a low, flat, earthfast boulder. Onto its smooth face has been cut remarkably intricate engraving. Rings containing cup marks, concentric circles and spirals all link together to form a striking design.

Carved deeply into the solid rock with only other rocks for tools, this was undoubtedly a work of great importance to the person or persons who created it. Whether it is art, or symbolism, or something beyond our understanding, it is truly amazing to sit beside it and wonder at its purpose and meaning. It isn't until you touch the rock that you might notice something unusual. It sounds hollow! In fact, the actual carving is now encased in a protective covering which is a perfect replica of it.

To my mind this is conservation at its best, protecting the original for the future, whilst still allowing the carving to be experienced in its natural setting. Carvings like this are rare, and ones as intricate are even rarer. In fact at least two others have been found on Gardom's Edge, and who knows what else might still be waiting to be found hidden beneath the moss and heather on the thousands of similar rocks scattered across the moor.

From the highpoint of the enclosure, a path leads out onto the enclosed fields which eat into its southern end. It drops down past a band of crags curling away from the edge itself to meet another track climbing up from the opposite direction. Another small enclosure is marked on some maps just a short distance further on, but I have never found it, merely a scattered collection of small clearance cairns.

Our route takes the new path, almost doubling back towards the enclosure, but after only a short distance it drops over the broken edge and descends into the boulder-strewn, oak woodland below it. This delightful path is followed as it runs below the cliffs, eventually leaving the trees before dropping down to the road.

Across the road the path continues, through a wooded dell, over an old packhorse bridge and steeply up through dense woodland until it rejoins our path out of Baslow at the old quarry below Baslow edge. This is a good place to sit and look back. Gardom's Edge stands out clear above the trees and it must look now very much as it did five thousand years ago to the travellers who were heading towards it. From the quarry back to Baslow is a pleasant reversal of the beginning of our route.

This is a marvellous walk. For anyone interested in the prehistory of the Peak District it is as good as it gets. If you do only one walk from this book, do this one!

8. Hob Hurst's House Beeley

Approx. distance: 5 miles

Approx. time: 3 hours

Starting point: Beeley GR 265677

Grade: A short but tricky walk over rough moorland

O.S. Maps: Explorer sheet OL 24; Landranger sheet 119

Grid references: Ring cairn GR 286684; Hob Hurst's House GR 287693; Beeley Warren stone circle GR 281685

The old estate village of Beeley is typical of the cluster of pretty villages which surround Chatsworth House. Built on the rising ground above the River Derwent, its mellow, stone cottages huddle around a far older Norman church. That in its turn sits beside an ancient, gnarled and hollow yew tree which must pre-date it by many centuries. Bypassed by the main road, the village is a tranquil haven, where vegetable gardens and horse paddocks are the rule rather than the exception. Above it, on the bleak moors which stretch away to the east are to be found a number of ancient sites, one of which, known as Hob Hurst's House, is unlike any other prehistoric site in the country.

The walk begins in the centre of the village beside the church, and takes the lane running eastwards, following the line of a stream flowing down from the hills towards the river. Only a short distance beyond the last few cottages, a track turns off the lane and climbs steadily towards an area of woodland filling the valley ahead. Plunging immediately into the wood, a pleasant path weaves through a mixture of tall pines, birch and beech trees. It crosses the stream on large stepping stones and rises steadily to where a steep zig-zag climbs up the head of the valley to arrive at a rough lane close to where it joins a moorland road.

Ahead, rugged moors sweep away in all directions, rising towards the dominant heights of Harland Edge which forms the eastern horizon. From its highpoint away to the south, the edge drops gradually down to the north, to where a high plantation of pines cloaks its upper slopes. On its broad crest, close to highest point of the woodland, sits Hob Hurst's House, the destination of our walk.

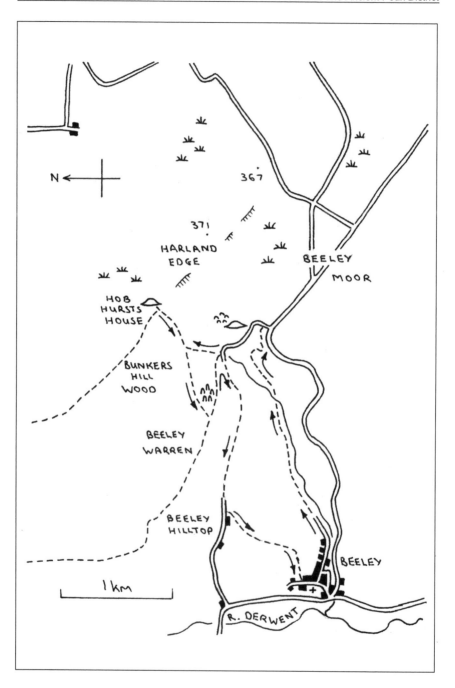

Turning along the lane, with the trees to the left and the moor to the right, you will soon reach a sharp left-hand bend. Just beyond it and over the high wall are several ancient sites. The nearest is a large heather covered tumulus, and just a short way beyond it a large ring cairn is hidden away in the grass. These can be visited, but be warned, the moor here is wet and the heather deep and even the short distance required to reach them can be testing!

At the next bend, a track branches off to the right, and almost immediately a footpath turns right off this, climbing up a shallow gully onto the moors.

This well-marked path rises steadily towards the high plantation. Away to the left, hidden in the folds of the moor, is the small Beeley Warren stone circle, but we will visit this on our way down from Hob Hurst's House. A metal footbridge crosses over a small stream, and a gate through the long wall splitting the moor soon brings you to an old packhorse track climbing up beside the woodland.

As the slope levels off, the trees end, and the broad ridge-top rises steadily to the right towards the crest of Harland Edge. Just beyond the last of the trees, within a protecting fence, is the very strange structure of Hob Hurst's house. A high earthen bank with an internal ditch encloses a square stone and earth barrow.

When it was first excavated in 1853 by local antiquarian Thomas Bateman, he found a square, stone-lined chamber within the barrow in which were human bones and charcoal. Unfortunately, the archaeological methods of the day were unable to date the remains and it is difficult now to place it into a particular period of prehistory. The stone cist would suggest a Bronze Age burial, but the surrounding banks and ditches should make it Neolithic, while its shape is typical of neither period. What is certain is that it is not only different but also much grander and more elaborate than the countless other cairns and barrows which are scattered over the surrounding moors.

One side of the structure has been eaten into by the packhorse trail which runs beside it, but other than that it remains largely intact. Its importance is indicated by the fact that it was one of the first monuments in the country to be given protection by English Heritage. Fortunately its remoteness has been its best protection, and, other than the rather intrusive pines of the nearby plantation and a farm track along the ridge, it remains a place of untouched solitude.

Whilst heading towards the barrow, an obvious question had sprung

Hob Hurst's House

to my mind. How had so old a place of burial come to be called Hob
Hurst's House? Fortunately a clue is given on a small plaque beside the
mound. Hob Hurst was the name given at some time in the more recent
past to a mythical elf who was supposed to have haunted the surrounding woods. I later discovered that a 'hob' is an old name for an evil spirit,
and a 'hurst' is a wooded hilltop. Perhaps this is old tale has been passed
down through the generations for thousands of years and is really a distant folk memories from ancient times. Were elves and sprites really
just scattered groups of indigenous people still living in the old Stone
Age ways in the woods and heaths? In the eyes of the new settlers they
were perhaps seen as a strange and mystical race who were to be
shunned and feared. The word 'pixie' is thought to come from the
Roman word 'picti' meaning 'the painted or tattooed people'! Perhaps
the tale of Hob Hurst is really as old as the strange mound that is named
after him!

   To return from his 'House' it is necessary to retrace your steps, following the old packhorse trail back down the steep bank alongside the
trees. However, once through the gate in the wall and over the metal
bridge, we take the path directly ahead instead of following the path to
the left that we came up on. This leads us up and over the lower moor,
which is known as Beeley Warren. Off to the left of the path in a slight
hollow is a stone circle which, despite the rather featureless nature of
the moor, is quite easy to miss.

   Although only a small circle, about fourteen paces across, it has

Beeley Warren stone circle

many interesting features. A ring of upright stones stand on the inner edge of a low stony bank. The uprights vary considerably in size, the tallest about four feet high, while some of the shorter ones barely raise themselves above the low bank. On the largest stone, which leans acutely, a large cup mark has been carved into its side. Some of the other uprights have fallen and lie partially buried in the grass, while others are missing completely, and it is difficult to tell how many there would have been originally.

Again, like so many of these small circles which are so characteristic of the East Moors, it is unclear if the uprights were a later addition to the circular bank, or vice versa, or if what we now see was the original design. Within the outer ring are also the remains of a later kerbed cairn, the kerb forming a secondary ring within the circle. It is most likely that what we see today is really the culmination of gradually evolving customs and beliefs over a period of many generations.

All over this lower moor there are signs that it once supported a thriving community. Enclosures, field systems and clearance cairns lie, largely buried, beneath the heather and grass of what is now a quiet and empty heath.

It is a wonderful place to sit, amongst the stones of the circle, away from the paths and largely ignored by the few passing walkers, and to simply enjoy the solitude. Only my last visit, the sun was shining on a still February day. Strips of snow still lined the shadows of the wall crossing the moor, but the chill east wind which had driven me down from Hob Hurst's House, had quietened. Only the occasional 'whirr' of the grouse broke the silence.

After returning to the path, it is only a short distance to where it joins a good track crossing the moor. Our route follows it back towards Beeley Woods, passing on the way a line of clearance cairns, to arrive back at the lane skirting the edge of the wood. Instead of simply retracing our steps back down through the woods, a pleasant alternative is to continue along the lane towards the old house at Beeley Hilltop. The route soon breaks clear of the trees and gives wonderful views down into the Derwent Valley, the tall spire of Edensor Church standing out prominently.

From the old farmhouse, a footpath cuts through the farmyard and follows a track out onto high fields to the top of a long slope with the village of Beeley below. The path down is a fine finish to the walk, following a line of old stone stiles and heading into the evening sun to arrive back in the centre of the village.

9. Stanton Moor
Stanton in Peak

Approx. distance: 4 miles

Approx. time: 2 hours

Starting point: Stanton in Peak GR 241643

Grade: A short and straightforward walk along lanes and good footpaths

O.S. Maps: Explorer sheet OL 24; Landranger sheet 119

Grid references: Andle Stone GR 240630; Doll Tor stone circle GR 238628; Cork Stone GR 244628; ring cairn GR 248633; Nine Ladies stone circle GR 249635; King Stone GR 248635

The village of Stanton in Peak climbs up the hillside above the valley of the River Lathkill. Above the last of the stone cottages, the high, wooded heathland of Stanton Moor stretches away to the south. Over the last hundred years the edges of the heath have been eaten into by quarries, but at its centre it remains one of the best preserved, Bronze Age burial grounds in the country.

The walk starts in the centre of the village, where the old hall, the pub and the church form a traditional hub to this old settlement. Cottage gardens, small paddocks and a wonderfully sloping cricket pitch complete the idyllic setting. It follows the lane out to the south which leaves the village and skirts around the edge of the moor in the direction of the next village of Birchover. To the right of the lane the land sweeps down into the wide shallow valley of the Ivy Bar Brook. Beyond it Youlgrave, with its tall, spired church is clearly visible in the valley, below wooded slopes which rise to Harthill Moor. To the left the birch-clad slopes of the old quarry workings climb up towards Stanton Moor.

The lane dips then rises to a wooded col, and just beyond it, the Andle Stone appears about a hundred metres away to the right. This huge single block of gritstone is perched on the edge of the slopes falling away into the valley. It is now surrounded by fields, hemmed in by rhododendron bushes and ringed by an old stone wall, but it must once have risen above the wooded valley like an island in a sea of trees.

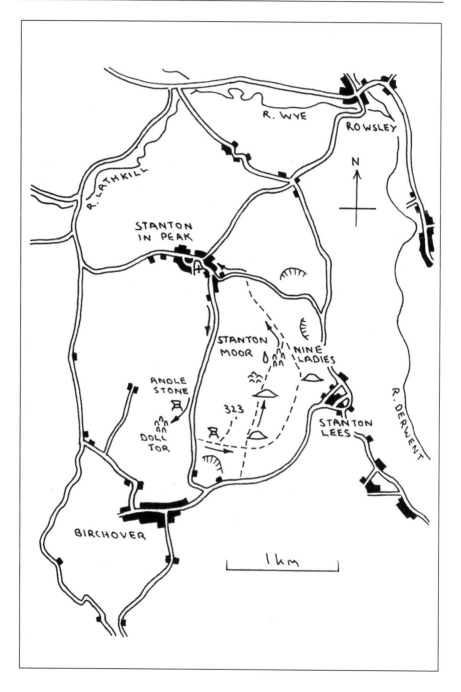

This natural feature would have been a very prominent landmark from the earliest of times and would almost certainly have come to be seen as a significant, and perhaps even sacred, place.

Originally very difficult to climb, a line of steps has, at some time in the past, been cut into the vertical face of the rock, and in more recent times a line of iron handholds has also been added to make the accent possible if still not easy. Its level top is covered with carvings which are predominantly relatively recent, but intermingle with several deep, circular, water-filled hollows which might well be much more ancient.

The surrounding view has little that prehistoric man would now recognise other than the slope of the land, but it is a fascinating place to try to reconstruct the landscape as it might once have been. The high moor behind, perhaps surmounted with burial cairns, and the densely wooded valley below, might well have been separated by scattered settlements and small fields. The tiny stone circle of Doll Tor, which is now hidden in a modern plantation would then have been clearly visible below the stone.

To visit this circle it is necessary to descend the stone, much trickier than climbing up, and cross the next small field to the pine woods in its far corner. A gate gives access to a track running along the edge of the plantation, and the circle is easily located a short way along it in the fringes of the wood.

This little gem of a circle has been accurately reconstructed in recent years, following a disastrous 'remodelling' in 1994. Six tiny uprights, linked by a continuous ring of smaller stones, surround a levelled platform, five paces long and four across. At its eastern end are the remains of a small cairn with a rectangular, stone cist within it. Later cremations were found to have been added to both the cairn and the stone circle.

Small by even Bronze Age standards, this site was probably a ritual site used by a single family or very small community. Its situation, just below and originally within sight of the Andle Stone, is no coincidence. The much older, natural 'altar' could well have been a focus for community worship for many generations before the small circle was built.

It should be noted that both the Andle Stone and Doll Tor are on privately owned land, but access seems to be accepted and an information board has been put up for visitors beside the small stone circle. Despite this, never take access for granted and always treat the land with respect.

After returning to the road, it is followed for only another hundred

Nine Ladies stone circle

metres to where a well marked path leads up onto the open 'Access' land of Stanton Moor. The path climbs up the wooded slope to where old quarries have eaten away into the edge of the heath. Beside the path is the strangely shaped Cork Stone, a natural free-standing pillar of gritstone. Standing about twelve feet high, it rises from a narrow base to a broad flat top. Again this can only be gained by a strenuous climb up the overhanging face with the aid of iron handholds. Carved into the top is a deep, and perfectly circular hollow. Like other such water-filled basins it is difficult to say just how old it is, but its size, its mirror-like reflection of the sky, and its inaccessibility would all suggest that it had some very ancient significance.

Beyond the Cork Stone it is possible to wander at will over the heath, and for those with time it is a fascinating place to explore. Over seventy burial cairns and mounds have been recorded here, and at one time at least four stone circles stood on the moor. Unfortunately, only a small fraction of these remain to be seen today, but they are enough to show us what an important site this must once have been.

For those with restricted time the best route is to follow the path past the Cork Stone, over the crest of the heath and then turn left onto the main track running up the broad back of the moor.

The King's Stone

Alongside this track are two of the best preserved cairns, although even these are badly damaged. Just beyond the second one and off to the left of the path is a large ringcairn. Its stony bank is over twenty-five paces across, but is mostly overgrown with heather now. Two narrow entrances can still be clearly made out, one facing north and one facing south. The one to the south is walled with vertical retaining stones. In the centre of the ring are what appear to be the remains of another cairn.

Beyond the ringcairn, the open heathland of heather and bilberry and gorse gives way to scattered birch woodland. Not far into it is the one remaining stone circle, the much celebrated Nine Ladies of Stanton Moor. This beautiful little circle is, despite its name, made up of ten surviving stones and at least one more is missing. One of the ten has fallen and none of the others stand above three feet high. They are linked by a low earthen bank, which might originally have had two entrances. The remains of a low cairn can just be made out in the centre. About thirty metres away to the west is the tiny outlying stone known as the King Stone. This much battered and scarred stone was broken by a car many years ago, but has been lovingly repaired and restored to the vertical.

Standing in the centre of a wide clearing ringed by wispy birches the setting is perfect. Perhaps this is the reason why this site, above all

others in the area, continues to be a site of seasonal worship and cele-
bration. The surrounding woods are dotted with the blackened circles
of camp fires and a small oak beside the circle is always adorned with a
strange assortment of tokens and offerings.

For this reason alone it is all the more sad that the site is continually
threatened by attempts to reopen the nearby quarries, which if allowed,
could encroach to within a hundred metres of this most beautiful and
spiritual monument.

From the circle the path continues through the woods to their edge,
then follows it along past the now overgrown scars of old quarries to
reach open fields. The view to the north is already blighted by new
quarry workings, which just serve to show how destructive further
development could be to Stanton Moor itself. The path crosses the
fields to a lane which runs down through woods and past the cricket
pitch to the outskirts of Stanton in Peak.

The great Bronze Age Necropolis of Stanton Moor has survived
because its heathland has been of little value agriculturally over the
intervening millennia. Although the surviving monuments are small
and only represent a fraction of what once existed, the whole area
remains a national treasure, and should be treated as such. Even if the
quarries left the stones themselves unharmed, they would undoubtedly
destroy the serene yet fragile environs of the Nine Ladies. Few who visit
this tiny circle fail to sense that it is indeed an unspoilt place, a special
place, seemingly untouched by the modern world. How sad that it
could be ruined so thoughtlessly!

10. Harthill Moor
Elton

Approx. distance: 4 miles

Approx. time: 2-3 hours

Starting point: Elton GR 222609

Grade: An excellent short walk along well-marked paths, with a short scramble to reach the top of Robin Hood's Stride

O.S. Maps: Explorer sheet OL 24; Landranger sheet 119

Grid references: Castle Ring GR 221628; Nine Stone Close GR 225626; Robin Hood's Stride GR 225623; Cratcliff Rocks GR 227624

Harthill Moor is a high gritstone plateau which rises like an island above the limestone of the White peak. Ringed by steep slopes and rocky edges, its undulating top is now mostly farmland, but enough evidence has survived to show us that it has been an important centre of settlement and ritual which dates back to the very beginning of Man's incursions into these uplands.

Standing up above the eastern rim of the plateau is a dramatic rocky tor, known as Robin Hood's Stride, which is the most visible and striking natural feature in the whole area. From the very earliest of days it would have been a prominent feature, and would over time have developed into a place of some significance where people might meet, or where camps would be set up each year. A number of shallow caves and shelters in the jumbled rocks of the tor, and along the line of the nearby crags, might well have added to its importance.

As the millennia passed, and farming brought a new stability to the people of the area, the rocks seem to have retained their importance. Carved into the surfaces of many of the rocks are many cup and ring marks. These mysterious designs, usually either a single ring, a shallow, circular hollow or a combination of the two, are still not really understood. Probably more to do with ritual than with any artistic or practical function, these strange, evocative signs are to be found all over the tor, intermingled with the graffiti of more modern times.

This short walk begins in Elton, a sleepy village of old stone cottages.

The route starts down a lane beside the church, and out onto open fields before dropping quickly down to a quiet road running northwards towards Harthill Moor. It follows the road for a few metres to a sharp bend where a track turns off into the woods. A natural spring amongst the trees has created a wet area where flag irises and campions surround a shallow pool, which overflows into a line of old gritstone water troughs. The path climbs through the woods, passing an old quarry and breaks out into open pasture land beyond.

Up ahead is a dramatic gritstone crag, one of a line marking the edge of the plateau. The path continues below the edge, following a line of lovely stone stiles, before climbing up between two of the outcrops onto the moor above. Although predominantly farmland, Harthill Moor is dominated by the natural features of the landscape, which still show through the thin veneer of modern agriculture. Just to the right of the path, close to an old stone barn is a low rise which is littered with large earthbound blocks of stone lying in a chaotic jumble. This is a marvellous viewpoint looking out to the purple line of the East Moors ringing the horizon. Nearer at hand are the earthworks of Castle Ring and, rising out of the trees, the rocky towers of Robin Hood's Stride.

From there the path passes through a thin belt of Scot's pine and beech, and crosses fields to join a farm track leading down off the northern edge of the plateau. The town of Youlgrave suddenly appears, spread out like a map in the valley below, its houses huddled around its old church. The track continues down towards it, but our route turns off to the right across fields, heading in the direction of Robin Hood's Stride.

When the path reaches a small patch of woodland it joins another track which turns sharply away to the north, towards Castle Ring clearly visible now on its hilltop. The path runs to the left of the hill to pick up the Limestone Way, which climbs the steep slope to the earthworks.

Despite the rather unfriendly notices, it is possible to view the single ditch and stone bank which surrounds this small, level enclosure. Often described as a hillfort, this structure is much too small to warrant such a description, and remains something of an enigma. Possible a defended homestead, it is thought to date from the end of the Bronze Age, but like many such enclosures it is possible that it has been superimposed onto a much older site.

From the Ring, the path skirts around the farm which now eats into

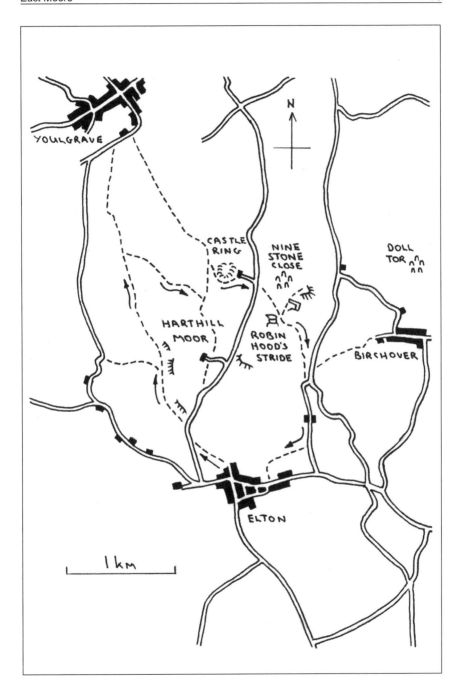

Nine Stones Close

the eastern arc of the ditch, and along its drive to rejoin the lane crossing the moor. This is crossed, and a path heads in the direction of the Stride, but before it is reached the dramatic stones of Nine Stone Close appear in a field to the left.

Despite their name only five stones remain, but what stones they are! Standing almost eight feet high, these gritstone giants have wonderfully fluted tops created by thousands of years of rainwater cascading down their weathered faces. Originally a circle, possibly of nine stones, although never more than seven have ever been recorded, four stand in their original position, while a fifth now acts as a gatepost in the nearby wall. The missing stones were said to be smaller than those that remain, although one visitor in 1799 describes a stone of seventeen feet still standing in the circle! These stones are much larger than the other circle stones still to be found in the peak, with the exception of those of Arbor Low. It is likely that it is a much earlier circle, probably dating from the late Neolithic period.

Its close proximity to Robin Hood's Stride is also no coincidence. The great natural rock temple is almost certainly the reason for the circle being built where it was. Anyone who stood within the circle at midsummer four thousand years ago would have seen the full moon framed exactly between the two towers of the Stride. This offers us a fascinating insight into their beliefs, which would appear to link their man-made temples with the natural features of the landscape, and also shows the importance of the moon in their customs and rituals.

Leaving the circle behind, it is only a short walk to the rocky tor and a quick scramble up to the foot of the towers themselves. To gain the actual summits of either of them is tricky, and coming down is even harder, so it is better to explore around them rather than attempting to scale them.

Many of the surrounding rocks have ancient cup and ring marks engraved in them. Some are still sharp and clear, others faded and can only be seen in a favourable light, but there are many of them interspersed amongst the carving of more recent times. Perhaps they were carved for the same reason, the intention to leave a mark that would outlive the carver. Perhaps it was more the physical act of carving, the rhythmical beating of the stone that was important, rather than the carving itself. Or was it simply an act of faith, much as we light a candle today, or sign a book of remembrance? Whatever their meaning or pur-

Robin Hood's Stride

pose, they mark the Stride as a special place, an ancient place and one which has been an important feature in the lives of the people of the area for many thousands of years.

From the main track, another path leads off to the east, along a line of broken cliffs to Cratcliff Rocks. The steep crags below conceal a number of shallow caves and rock shelters that were probably well known to the prehistoric people who lived on the moor. At their top is a wonderful area of enormous blocks of stone, piled in chaotic heaps, and overgrown with heather, bilberries and ferns. Stunted oaks, rowans and birch trees form a broken canopy over the rocks and a maze of narrow paths wind over and through them. On the slope leading back down to Nine Stones Close is an enclosure, where earthen banks link a number of natural earthfast rocks, and encloses what is thought to be several hut platforms. It is now difficult to locate as it uses the natural features of the land, but it is probably a rare example of a settlement site dating from the Neolithic period.

After exploring this fascinating area, our route returns to the main trail which drops down between the Stride and Cratcliff Rocks to a farm track leading towards the road below. There are good views back up towards the sheer cliffs behind, and ahead to where the village of Winster nestles in the folds of the hills.

The track joins a narrow lane which climbs up and away from the main road, passing the stone buildings of Dudwood Farm. It then enters a green tunnel of overhanging trees arching over a wonderful variety of woodland plants growing in their shade, including the beautiful blue flowers of the larkspur which flowers in the early summer. A path then turns off to the right, contouring steeply up and around the hillside. There are good views behind, looking back over Harthill Moor, with the Stride and Cratcliff Rocks still rising dramatically out of the trees. When the path levels off, it skirts around the village cricket pitch and re-enters the village of Elton.

The White Peak

Minninglow

11. Demons' Dale
Taddington

Approx. distance: 5 miles

Approx. time: 3 hours

Starting point: Taddington GR 146710

Grade: A complex, and at times muddy walk, but with plenty of interest along the way and in spring, a riot of colour.

O.S. Maps: Explorer sheet OL 24; Landranger sheet 119

Grid references: settlement site GR 168703; Demon's Dale rock shelter GR 169704; Fin Cop GR 175710; burial cairn GR 168710

Near to the village of Taddington, the River Wye twists through a deep and narrow gorge as it flows eastwards towards the Derwent Valley. The steep, wooded flanks are broken by a number of short, but steep, side valleys which cut down from the high limestone plateau on either side. Where two of these, Deep Dale and Demons' Dale, meet is a small triangular piece of flat ground on a low shelf above the main valley. This parcel of sheltered, level land has been used and visited by our ancestors for at least eight thousand years.

To reach it we begin our walk in Taddington, a long and narrow village tucked away beneath the high, bleak pastures of Taddington Moor. By-passed by the main road, it remains a working, farming settlement, and seems to have escaped the 'gentrification' suffered by many of the Peak District villages. Of interest is the fact that it consists of only one road, but the many tracks and paths leading off it are all named. The rather grand-sounding Dokindale Road seems to be no more than a narrow path running away into the fields.

Our route follows the main street out of the village eastwards, as it climbs up through small, walled fields ringed by ash trees. As it levels out, a left turn leads past a row of cottages and on to the isolated house at Taddington Field. A footpath drops down below the house and follows a muddy track down into the dale bottom. Closely hemmed in by low, overhanging trees, this rather claustrophobic dale is followed down until it is possible to escape along a ramp which branches off to the

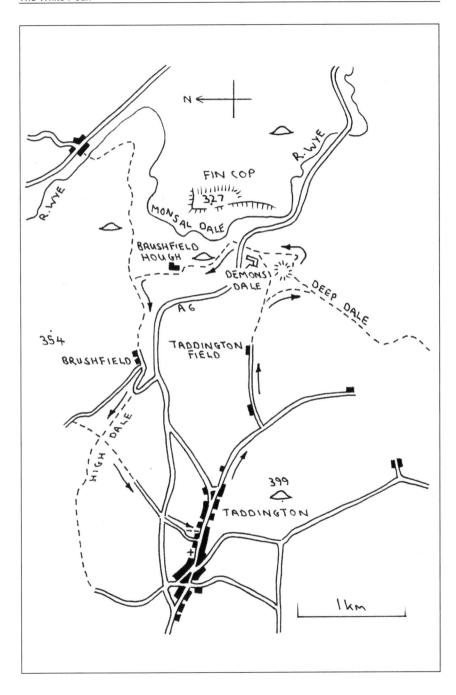

right. This turn is unmarked and easy to miss, but is the first track climbing up from the valley floor. It traverses around the hillside, through coppiced hazelwoods, before dropping down into Deep Dale.

This wonderful dale should be visited in the spring, when it is awash with wild flowers. Literally millions of cowslips cover the hillsides, with early purple orchids and other rare, lime-loving plants in abundance. Now preserved as a nature reserve, it is a wonderful place to wander and admire the spectacular plant life which is often hidden away in these deep and secretive dales.

Instead, our route turns back down the valley, crosses over the stream which can be tricky after rain, and contours around the hillside towards the main Wye Valley. On the end of this spur is a small area of level ground. Above it the wooded slopes rise to rocky, limestone crags and pinnacles, while below, the deep cleft of Demons' Dale cuts down to the main valley. Across the valley rises the great prow of high ground known as Fin Cop, on which a late Bronze Age promontory fort almost certainly rests on even older settlements.

This small triangle of land has many advantages as a place to live. It is sheltered, has a good supply of water, and deep fertile soil. It also has something else which would have made it an important place in prehistoric times. In a long, low outcrop of limestone above the river are bands of black chert, a very hard flint-like rock which was ideal for the making of stone blades and tools.

The remains of a small settlement are immediately obvious. A walled enclosure and the base of several buildings can still be easily traced as moss-covered, stone banks covering the centre of the clearing. These date from the late Iron Age, and could have been used right up to the time of the Romans, but other finds on the site would suggest that it was used for many thousands of years before that.

It is easy to see where the chert has been quarried and it is worth searching amongst the many mole hills on the site for broken tools or worked blades. I remember well the amazing feeling when I picked up a small, but exquisitely tooled, flint scraper lying on a small mound of newly excavated soil. To pick it up and realize that it probably hadn't been touched since it was dropped or discarded, perhaps, six or seven thousand years ago, was very strange. I couldn't help but wonder who had made it, and as it slotted comfortably into my fingers, what it had last been used for. Had it skinned the evening's meal, or cut through the tough sinews of a deer to make a string for a bow?

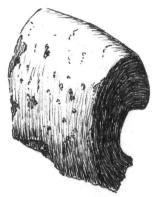

Iron Age pottery and Mesolithic blade from Demon's Dale

The person who had made it would have been a Mesolithic hunter, perhaps one of a small group living in the sheltered dale over the winter. Perhaps they would have carried a collection of such tools, each a treasured possession, and its loss would have been felt. Perhaps it was too small and not comfortable to use and it was simply thrown away and another made.

Near to the scraper I also found a small fragment of a pot, a piece of the rim of a 'gritted ware' bowl, which was probably made in the late Iron Age and used by the people who had lived and farmed in the small settlement still visible on the site. It is fascinating to think that these two chance finds, lying within feet of each other, are both evidence of prehistoric activity in the dale, but one predates the other by perhaps five thousand years. To the man who made the pot, the small blade would, even then, be older to him than Stonehenge is to us!

Not far away is another site that adds more pieces to the strange jigsaw puzzle of this valley, and suggests that the area might also have been used in the intervening periods.

To reach it, the path is followed past the settlement to join another track turning down the steep slope to where the stream tumbles out of the narrow gorge of Demons' Dale. It then crosses the stream, and leads around a spur of high ground before opening up into the main valley. At the foot of the broken slopes to the left of the path is a low cave mouth. Within this small rock shelter were found the remains of at least four people, buried in Neolithic times along with a flint knife and a number of chert tools. Broken pottery from both the Bronze Age and the Roman period were also discovered.

Demon's Dale rock shelter

When taken all together, the diverse evidence paints a picture of a place that was used and lived in for thousands and thousands of years. It is only in the post-Roman period that the site seems to have been abandoned. Perhaps too remote and isolated from the newer settlements, it became used only as marginal grazing land between the encroaching woodlands. Thankfully, it is this which has helped to preserve it.

From the rock shelter it is a short walk along the path to the car park beside the main A6. After crossing over the road the footpath forks, the right-hand path leading on into Monsal Dale, while our path climbs steeply up to the left, through the woods towards Brushfield.

As it breaks out of the trees at the top of the slope, the whole of the Wye Valley opens up behind. Fin Cop dominated the view to the east, its natural west-facing defences hiding its man-made earthworks on the more gentle eastern slopes. Directly below, our small settlement site at the bottom of Demon's Dale is clearly visible. Just beside the path is an ancient cairn. A thicket of gnarled and twisted hawthorns now sprout from the rocky mound, but it must originally have commanded a marvellous view over the valley.

The path then follows the crest of the ridge towards a range of magnificent but rather dilapidated farm buildings at Brushfield Hough, passes through the farmyard and out along a muddy lane onto high fields. At a large hollow ash tree it joins a rough lane which runs along the wooded edge of Taddington Dale to the small hamlet of Brushfield. The lane continues, signposted now for Taddington, and drops down into the narrow valley of High Dale.

Our route then leaves the road and takes a footpath up the dale, following the line of the usually dry streambed until another path climbs steeply up to the left, zig-zagging up the slope to reach a stile and a signpost pointing across small, walled fields in the direction of Taddington. Before long this path reaches a 'green lane' which is followed to the main road. Once over the busy duel-carriageway it is only a short distance back into the centre of the village.

Few places in the Peak District, in fact in the whole of England, display such a range of evidence suggesting a continuity of settlement over such a vast period of time. Even its name is intriguing. 'Demons' Dale' as it suggests, is a place supposedly haunted by demons. It is fascinating how many truly ancient places have become associated with such stories. Perhaps it does indeed retain something from its long history, something which we feel but don't understand and therefore fear. Perhaps the man, who carefully chipped away at the small flint blade all those thousands of years ago, can still rest his hand on your shoulder as you sit amongst the ancient stones of Demon's Dale!

12. High Wheeldon Longnor

Approx. distance: 6 miles

Approx. time: 3-4 hours

Starting point: Longnor GR 089649

Grade: A fascinating walk through fine scenery, using quiet lanes and well-marked footpaths. The ascent of High Wheeldon involves a steep climb. Access to Dowel Cave involves a short scramble, and permission is required to enter Fox Hole Cave.

O.S. Maps: Explorer sheet OL 24; Landranger sheet 119

Grid references: High Wheeldon GR 100662; Fox Hole Cave GR 099663; Dowel Cave GR 075676

Forming the northern slopes of the upper Dove Valley is a line of spectacular limestone hills. Thousands of years of ice, rain and wind have carved them into shapely peaks with narrow ridges and tottering pinnacles. Between them, a series of steep-sided gorges drop down from high upper valleys to the main valley floor. Streams emerge from ancient springs and caves plunge deep into the hillsides.

In some of these caves, hidden away in the broken slopes of these hills, early Man took shelter. Over thousands of years he came to look upon them as special places, places of significance that gave access to the Great Earth Mother. They were to become their tombs, secretive places hidden away and known only to a few, where their dead could be buried with dignity and ritual.

Our walk begins in Longnor, a beautiful, old town which sits on a narrow gritstone ridge separating the upper valleys of the Dove and the Manifold. Just off the busy main street, lovely old houses of mellow stone and narrow winding lanes cluster around a cobbled central square. At the last of the houses, at the eastern end of the village, is a narrow lane which runs to the edge of the Dove Valley, before dropping down into it.

Ahead there is a wonderful view across the very different landscape of the limestone ridges which form the far side of the valley. High Wheeldon Hill stands directly across the valley, its steep conical slopes

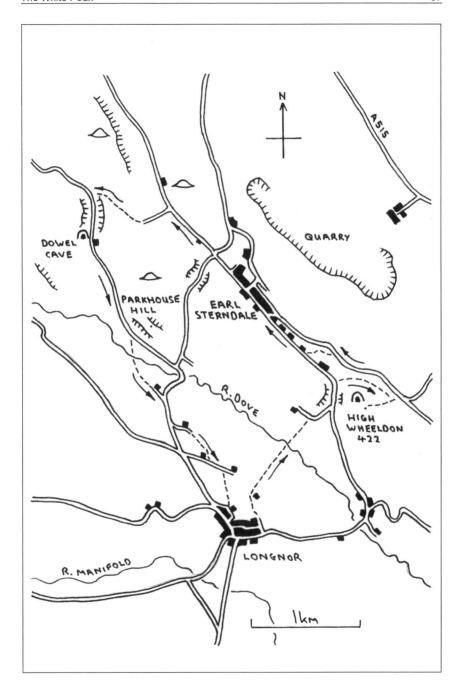

rising to a sharp summit, its smooth flanks giving no indication of the secret place that it has hidden within it. To its left, a long ridge rises and falls before breaking into the shattered crests of Parkhouse Hill and Chrome Hill – the latter is probably derived from old English 'crum' (and modern Welsh) 'crwm' meaning 'crooked' or 'bent', referring to the shape of the hill. Between these two ridges, and hidden away in the folds of the hills behind them, is the steep gorge where Dowel Cave lies hidden and forgotten.

The lane leads to a stone barn, where a footpath climbs briefly before dropping down to the River Dove winding through a narrow wooded dell. Beyond it, a grassy lane bordered by an expanse of wild flowers climbs gently to join a tiny lane heading towards High Wheeldon. As the lane skirts around its broad base, the smooth slopes above still conceal any hint of its hidden secret. The route follows the lane through the narrow defile separating High Wheeldon from the adjacent hill, until a path turns off to the right. This climbs around the back of the hill to join the main path which climbs directly up the steep slopes towards the summit. Several broken bands of rock run across the slope, and the line of ascent winds through them to reach the trig point perched on the top, and a view unrivalled in the whole of the Peak.

A narrow ridge drops away to the north-west to where one of the bands of rock breaks through the grassy slopes, and there, hidden away and partially concealed by a clump of nettles, is Fox Hole Cave. The entrance, although very small, is in fact slightly larger than it was originally because it was enlarged to assist the rescue of a trapped dog back in the 1920s. A barred, iron gate now closes off the cave system below, but permission to enter, and a key, can be obtained in advance from the South Peak Estate Office by phoning 01335 350503.

Behind the gate is a short drop into a small chamber, from where a narrow passage leads to a second slightly larger chamber. Beyond another constriction is a third chamber, with three final passages forming a cruciform pattern leading away from it. Those to the left and straight ahead quickly become too low to allow easy passage, but the righthand passage dives steeply down and winds around several muddy bends before rising to a final tiny chamber. This eerie and atmospheric place has a magnificent vaulted roof from which a narrowing chimney disappears into the darkness above. If ever there was a place of entry into a mystical underworld it is surely to be found there.

Most of the human remains were discovered in the outer sections of

Entrance to Fox Hole Cave

the system, but finds of stone artefacts, worked bones and the charcoal stains of ancient hearths continued deep within the cave. A further indication of human activity is a bear's vertebra which had been hollowed out to use as a lamp. Some of the worked stones and animal bones date from as far back as the Palaeolithic, although the human remains are all thought to be from the Neolithic.

Why were they buried there, in a tiny hole hidden away, deep inside a high hill that in Neolithic times would probably have been further concealed by a thick covering of vegetation? Possibly the cave had always been known as a 'special place', and one which therefore conferred importance to the bodies buried there. The inaccessibility of the cave would suggest that it was never a place of habitation, and so the large number of hearths so deep below ground must suggest that they were the result of rituals carried out within the cave. Evidence from other caves suggest that offerings, in the form of small reptiles, bats or special plants, were burnt in the fires as a part of these ceremonies. Perhaps these were associated with their beliefs in an 'Earth Mother', and these were offerings to her. Perhaps the fact that it was a secluded, hidden place gave it added importance, because only those that knew of its existence could share in its secrets.

We will never know why the bodies were buried there, or what rituals actually took place, but the cave certainly retains its unique atmosphere. Just to sit outside the tiny entrance, looking out along the rocky spine of hills stretching away into the distance, is a humbling experience. To actually sit on the cool clay inside one of the dark, water-smoothed inner chambers, lit only by the flicker of a tiny lamp, is completely and utterly overwhelming.

To continue the walk, the summit of high Wheeldon must again be gained and the path taken back down to the road. This is then followed for a short way until a track cuts off to the left, and drops down to a lower and much quieter lane leading into Earl Sterndale. This is a sleepy little settlement with a lovely stone Hall, ancient cottages and a quaint pub surrounding a small village green on which chickens strut and peck at the ground.

After passing through the village, the lane crosses over the main road from Buxton to Longnor, and begins to climb back into the hills towards Axe Edge. Wonderful views open up to the left of the lane, the pinnacled edges of Chrome Hill and Parkhouse Hill prominent in the foreground. The route continues past the strangely named house of Hatch-a-Way until a footpath leads off to the left, passing around the top of a dry valley to join a farm track leading up towards the long ridge of Upper Edge. As it reaches the shoulder of the hill, a path curls away to the right, and after a short rise, drops quickly down into a narrow limestone gorge.

Running through it is a quiet lane, above which the broken crags rise steeply. When I last visited, it was a cloudless day in June, and each isolated hawthorn tree cast a deep shadow into which the sheep had clus-

Dowel Cave

tered to escape the sun. The white rocks shimmered in the heat and were splashed with the vivid red of herb robert that grew in tangles along the ledges and terraces of the crags. Even the jackdaws had paused their incessant metallic cries and were huddled in silent groups in the few trees which sprouted precariously from the upper cliffs.

Dowel Cave is difficult to locate at first, and it is only as you are about to leave the lower end of the gorge, that its small shadowy entrance can be seen high up to the right beneath over-hanging trees. It can be reached through a metal gate, and a short but steep scramble up the rather overgrown slope falling away from the cliffs above.

The entrance is small, and behind it a passage descends down into the hillside. After a short initial drop, it levels out into a small chamber, beyond which the roof lowers and the passage narrows considerably. Beyond this constriction, the passage drops steeply again to further chambers. Most of the human remains were found in the outer section of the cave, where the jumbled bones of at least seven people and two dogs were found. Six of the human skulls were purposefully placed against the right-hand wall, some surrounded by stones and all facing into the cave. One of the skulls had a strange, worn hole in it, which suggested that it had been carried on the end of a spear or stick before being interred in its final resting place. An ox bone and several flint blades were found with them.

In the narrow section beyond, a wall of stones blocked the passage, and there were two further inhumations behind it. Further in again, another wall closed off the inner cave where the skull of a child was placed beside a selection of ox bones.

The cave can be entered, but beyond the first narrow chamber the passage is very constricted and the floor drops away steeply and unexpectedly. Exploration beyond there should be attempted only by the very experienced. Again, it is sufficient to sit outside the narrow entrance and let the imagination explore its inner depths, and the unknown rituals which must have taken place there.

From the cave the lane is followed out of the gorge, passing another small opening out of which flows a small stream, and out into a huge natural amphitheatre enclosed by the dramatic ridges of Chrome Hill and Parkhouse Hill. The lane runs through a narrow gap between these two hills which is marked by a huge pinnacle standing like a sentinel guarding the entrance to the pass.

From there, a footpath leaves the lane, crosses over the River Dove and climbs around the back of an isolated house to reach the main road leading back into Longnor. The final section of the walk along this busy road can be avoided by turning off to the left, and following a series of farm tracks and footpaths which weave through the aptly named settlement of Under the Hill, before climbing back up to Longnor.

This is a tremendous walk, passing through some spectacular scenery, and it visits two of the most evocative and magical sites in the Peak District. Most of the landscape above ground has been changed by man to such an extent that envisaging the scenery and surroundings of five thousand years ago is very difficult. Below ground, in the narrow confines of Fox Hole and Dowel caves, nothing has changed, and one can experience the same sensations which first drew our distant ancestors to these secret and mysterious places.

13. Lathkill Dale
Over Haddon

Approx. distance: 7 miles

Approx. time: 3-4 hours

Starting point: Over Haddon GR 204664

Grade: a straightforward walk along lanes and well-marked footpaths. Permission is required to enter any caves in Lathkill Dale.

O.S. Maps: Explorer sheet OL 24; Landranger sheet 119

Grid references: Ringham Low GR 169664; Lathkill Head cave GR 170658; Calling Low rock shelter GR 184655

Lathkill Dale is one of those special places that seems to have been largely untouched by the modern world. It is true that on a sunny weekend in the summer, it is busy with walkers who follow the easy path along its stream, admiring the wild flowers and the woods. But in the early morning, the late of the evening, or when the winter winds sweep over the moors it is still possible to visit a landscape that our most ancient ancestors would find instantly recognisable.

It is quite likely that some of the very first men to ever reach as far north as the Peak District would have visited Lathkill Dale. They would have sheltered in its caves and rock shelters from the arctic winds of the plateau above, and would have marvelled at the hard black rock that they found in seams within the limestone cliffs. In those far off days of the Old Stone Age, the dale would have been a rock-strewn gorge of broken cliffs and steep scree slopes, offering a bleak but welcome shelter for the hunters who came each year following the herds of reindeer and bison who trekked north with the summer sun.

As the Ice Age drew to a close, the dale would have been slowly colonised by shrubs and trees. Birches and hawthorn bushes would have taken root in the deepening soil between the stones, and willows and alders in thickets along the banks of the stream. By the time that the great stones of Arbor Low were being raised just to the south, the gorge would have been thick with tall stands of ash and beech growing in its fertile microclimate.

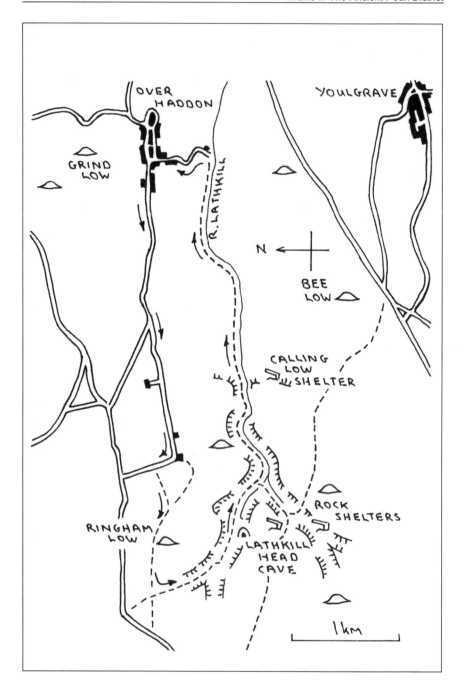

Today it is possible to see the dale in all these garbs. As you pass from the barren rocks of its upper reaches, through the open grasslands and scattered hawthorns of the central section, and into the dense woodland beside the lower river, it is like travelling through the last twelve thousand years of our history. And for those willing to look beyond the ephemeral beauty of the valley today, enough evidence can still be found to tell the tale of these ancient times.

We begin the walk in Over Haddon, up on the rich grasslands above the lower reaches of the gorge. It starts along the lane heading westwards towards Monyash. The land slopes away to the left, and the deep, wooded gorge of Lathkill Dale is clearly visible beyond the first fields. Before long the lane splits and the left-hand fork winds pleasantly along towards Haddon Grove, between very old hawthorn and elderberry trees. The springtime flowers are spectacular. Campions and bluebells cluster beneath tall stands of cow parsley and clumps of wild garlic hide in the shadows between the trees.

At Haddon Grove the road turns sharply right and this is taken for just a short way until a track turns off to the left across the fields. The route is easily followed over obvious stiles towards the large wooded copse on the crest of a low hill. This is Ringham Low, a once magnificent Neolithic chambered cairn. It originally contained at least five separate chambers, all entered through their own passageways, and covered in one large mound of stones. Similar in size and structure to Minninglow, its multiple chambers are unusual and could possibly have represented separate family tombs within a communal cairn.

Sadly, all that remains on the surface now is a scattering of loose stones within the walled copse and the hint of a surrounding ditch and bank. Despite the disappointment of its destruction, its site remains significant, as it sits up on a spur of land looking out over Lathkill Dale. It is one of at least six tumuli which ring the deep dale below.

The path continues over the fields, until it drops into a shallow dry valley known as Nandale, which leads down towards the head of Lathkill Dale. The low limestone outcrops on either side of the path increase in height until all of a sudden the main valley appears below, a great fissure cutting through the landscape. Tiers of broken cliffs rise above loose slopes of scree.

Here is the landscape of the Old Stone Age, and on a cold winter day it is quite easy to imagine mammoths and woolly rhinos grazing on the few bushes and stubby trees growing in the shelter of the gorge. Hyenas

Lathkill Head Cave

would have lived in the caves below, competing with the occasional
hunter for their shelter, while herds of wild horses, reindeer and bison
ranged across the open tundra above.

But when I last visited, the sun was shining on a fine spring day, the
ghosts of the mammoths were gone, and the valley was alive with may-
flowers and early purple orchids flowering in profusion among the scattered rocks. Gone too were the wild horses and the bison, replaced by a
scattering of plump sheep grazing the rough slopes.

The path drops down steeply to the main valley floor where a lovely
track winds between the rocks. It is up in the cliffs above that seams of
hard, black chert can still be found and has been dug out for as long as
men have been coming to the valley. Many early tools, blades and
scrapers, arrowheads and axes have been found crafted from this rock,
the best workable stone to be found in the area. One axe, carefully
crafted from the local stone, and dating from the Mesolithic Period, was
found carefully concealed inside a small rock fissure within the dale.

Not far along the valley is the first real cave, known as Lathkill Head

Cave. Opening below a band of overgrown cliffs, its large entrance quickly lowers to where it is almost blocked by large boulders. Beyond them it opens up for a short way. The water-smoothed rocks of its floor pay testament to its being the source of the River Lathkill during wet periods, and this would have precluded its use by early Man for anything more than a temporary shelter. A scattering of chert flakes and chippings, still to be found on its floor, would however suggest that it was used at least occasionally.

Beyond the cave the valley continues, deepening and gradually widening, until suddenly the stream appears from its more usual source beneath a large rock outcrop. Within a matter of metres, it becomes a substantial flow tumbling over rocks and adding its tinkling tones to the sound of the skylarks above. The path runs beside it until the small Sheepwash Bridge appears, which marks the point where two arms of the dale meet. The main valley continues to the east but it is worth making a short diversion into Cales Dale which, at this point, joins from the south.

This is the gorge as it has looked since Neolithic times. Thickly vegetated with hawthorns and ash trees, a natural path, worn only by the passing of feet, winds up the dale between steep slopes and broken cliffs. Higher up, the dale narrows and the cliffs become undercut, offering some protection from the weather. Little reliable archaeological evidence has survived, but it is almost certain that this side valley has been used for shelter by men since they first reached this far north. Near to One Ash Grange Farm, which can be reached by a very ancient track climbing up a short subsidiary valley, is one such rock shelter where a Neolithic burial, along with a knife blade, arrowhead and many flint flakes were in fact found at the beginning of the last century. The whole area is worth exploring, as it one of the few places which can be genuinely said to have remained largely unchanged for many thousands of years, and it is still possible to experience the dale as our earliest ancestors would have seen it.

After returning to the main valley, the easy path can now be pleasantly followed as it runs beside the stream. On the opposite bank, the sides of the dale are now thickly wooded with hawthorn and taller ash trees. The stream, lined with reeds, runs over several small waterfalls, and is alive with water birds. Mallards, coots and moorhens are everywhere, wagtails flit amongst the spray of the falls and dippers bob importantly on the rocky islands in mid-stream.

Rock shelters in Cales Dale

At the top of the steep slopes to the left, looking out over the gorge, are several burial cairns, which again underlines the significance that this dale had in ancient times.

The dale swings around to the right below impressive cliffs, passes several man-made weirs, and arrives at the point where two more side valleys join the main dale. The one off to the left is an open grassy dale lined with low cliffs. The one to the right is Calling Low Dale, and is filled with an almost impenetrable jungle of low scrub beneath a tall canopy of ash trees. Hidden within this valley, at the foot of a belt of tall cliffs, is Calling Low rock shelter.

When this was excavated, it was discovered that it contained the remains of a large number of burials from the Neolithic Period. These included the skeleton of a woman with a pierced skull, a woman with a young child and a group of six small children, all buried together. Assorted bones from a number of other individuals, together with pottery, arrowheads and chert blades were also found, and a human pelvis had been placed with a fox's skull in a small niche in the back wall.

Why the cave was chosen as a burial site is unclear, but it is almost certain that the side valley was then, as it is now, heavily wooded and very difficult to enter. It is possible that it was its hidden location and inaccessibility which gave it a mystique and a degree of secrecy that added significance to the burials and the rituals which were carried out there.

Today the shelter is beyond the reach of this walk, but it is perhaps a comforting thought that it remains the quiet and secluded place that it has probably been for most of the last five thousand years.

Beyond Calling Low Dale, the track continues alongside the river, which runs through the lovely woodland which now fills the widening valley. Tall beeches and elms begin to outnumber the ash trees, and in the sun-filled glades beside the river, wild flowers grow in profusion. The remains of old mill ponds and races and a scattering of ruined buildings among the trees, are now all that remain of a once thriving lead industry. They add another layer to the history of the dale and provide interest for the remainder of the route, which soon reaches Lathkill Lodge with its old clapper bridge over the river. From there a lane climbs steeply and quickly back up to Over Haddon and the end of the walk.

14. Arbor Low
Middleton

Approx. distance: 9 miles

Approx. time: 4-5 hours

Starting point: Middleton GR 196632

Grade: A long walk along easy to follow footpaths and trails, with several unavoidable sections along lanes.

O.S. Maps: Explorer sheet OL 24; Landranger sheet 119

Grid references: Roman road GR 166623; Arbor Low GR 161636; tumulus GR 162635; Gib Hill GR 158634; Bee Low GR 192647

On the rounded crest of a high ridge in the very centre of the White Peak stands one of the most significant prehistoric monuments in the north of England. On an ancient route which crossed between the deep valleys of the Dove and the Lathkill rivers, the great Neolithic complex of Arbor Low was raised almost five thousand years ago and remains one of the most dramatic and atmospheric sites in the Peak District.

This walk begins in Middleton, a lovely village of old stone cottages on a high shelf of land above the River Bradford. It initially takes the lane running west, up the long hill out of the village. At the last of the houses, and the beginning of the woods, a choice of routes is available. The most direct way is to continue along the tree-lined lane for about a mile, but for those wishing to take a more interesting, but circuitous, route, a narrow lane climbs steeply up to the left.

This takes you up into a delightful area of typical limestone hill country. Fields of buttercups enclosed by dry-stone walls, and a stony track bordered by a wild tangle of campion, yellow vetch and tiny speedwells, roll away over the hills, passing a few remote farms before dropping back down to a road. A wooded hill off to the left of the track, Kenslow Knoll, has two Bronze Age tumuli on its summit. The road is then taken northwards to rejoin the more direct route, where a farm lane turns off towards Mere Farm.

Passing the farm, a track continues up the hill, through a belt of

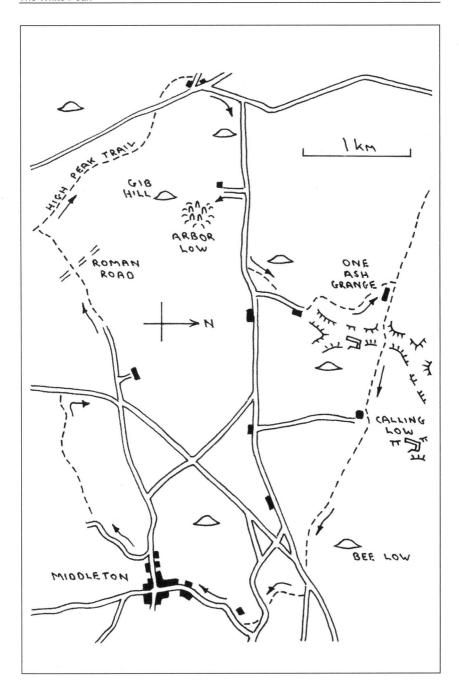

woodland, past an area of old mineral workings, before climbing once more to where the course of a Roman road is marked by the straight edge of a woodland belt. A plaque beside the track reads, 'Aquae Arnemetiae – Derventio', which indicates that it was the Buxton to Derby road. Further on, the line of the road passes within metres of the Arbor Low complex. What the young legionaries must have thought of the strange temple on its wind-swept hilltop can only be imagined. Beyond the Roman road the track, fringed with hawthorns, drops down into a wide and shallow valley.

At this point our route joins the High Peak Trail which follows the course of an old railway line, and now provides an easy route for riders, cyclists and walkers through the heart of the National Park. At first it runs along an embankment, with fine views across the low valley towards the ridge on which Arbor Low sits just out of sight. It is interesting to pick out the route of the Roman road running just below the crest of the ridge.

This section of the walk has the added pleasure of an abundance of wild life which is attracted by the rough verges which line the sides of the trail. In the late spring, yellow and purple vetch, clover and speedwell all add their colour to the tall grasses, banded snails creep across the path and skylarks hang in the sky. In the lush meadows to either side, curlews probe the ground with their long bills.

Away to the left is Lean Low, a Bronze Age barrow clearly visible beside the trig point on the crest of the hill.

Soon the trail passes through a belt of tall beech woodland before plunging into a deep, fern-lined cutting which leads beneath the main road and to the junction with the Tissington Trail. Just beyond it, the views to the west open up, the western moors darkly lining the horizon beyond the nearer limestone hills.

At Parsley Hay the route leaves the trail, crosses over the busy main road and turns onto the Long Rake, a lane which follows a line of old mineral works. Just beyond a patch of woodland is the site of another Bronze Age tumulus, now no more than a gentle rise in the field. A track off to the right leads to the farmhouse below Arbor low. It is requested that all visitors contribute 50p towards the maintenance of the site, which can be put in a small tin beside the farmhouse as you pass.

It is only a short walk up onto the open heath, but it is enough to add a feeling of isolation and remoteness which gives such an atmosphere to this marvellous place. The high bank of the henge is all that is seen at

Arbor Low

first, but as you enter through the obvious gap, the inner ditch and stone circle suddenly appear. The stones, all of locally-quarried limestone, now lie flat, but they must originally have been an imposing and dramatic sight as the henge was entered. It has been suggested that the bank was intended to create just this effect, shutting out all sight of the circle and the ceremonies which took place within it, from everyone outside.

The stones must have been tall, many well over ten feet in height, and even prone they create a dramatic effect, circling around the edge of the still-deep ditch, like the numbers on a clock face. At its centre are three more recumbent stones, all that remains of a central cove, an inner sanctum reminiscent of the one still standing at Avebury. A large mound in the bank beside the southern entrance is a Bronze Age barrow in which was found a stone cist containing a collection of human bones, some burnt, a bone pin, a piece of flint and two late Neolithic pots. From the outer bank, another earthwork curls away towards a tall tumulus known as Gib Hill, several hundred metres away, which sits on the site of a much older long barrow.

To understand more about this strange assortment of monuments, it is important to realise that the site gradually evolved over a period of several thousand years. Many artefacts, some dating back to the Mesolithic Period, have been found scattered across the hilltop, marking it as a place of importance even before the first surviving structure was constructed, possibly as a settlement site or a seasonal encampment. Then the long barrow was built, followed several hundred years later by the henge and the linking earthwork. The circle stones and central cove were added later, possibly replacing an earlier timber circle. Gib Hill Barrow then replaced the long barrow and the great mound was added to the bank of the henge. Finally, after the site had probably been abandoned throughout the Iron Age, the Romans ran their road past the already ancient temple.

There are many theories why none of the stones still stand. Some have suggested that they never did, but it seems more likely that the brittle nature of the rock combined with the weather was responsible. It is also possible that it was a case of wanton destruction at a later date by people trying to destroy the power of the stones and what they represented. Their influence continues, however, and the site remains one of the most atmospheric and evocative places I know.

Central cove of Arbor Low

After returning to the road, it is followed eastwards until a marked footpath turns off to the left, cutting across fields to a farm track. This passes Cales Farm, skirts around the head of a limestone gorge descending into Lathkill Dale and continues to One Ash Grange Farm, where it joins the Limestone Way. From its lovely old range of farm buildings, the route drops steeply down into the gorge along an ancient pitched pathway.

Hidden away within the dale are several rock shelters used by Mesolithic hunters for shelter, and by their Neolithic descendants as secret places of burial and ritual. It is a fascinating area to explore. It is possible that the eventual siting of Arbor Low was influenced by an ancient trackway which crossed from here to the deep gorges of the Dove and the Manifold away to the west.

The route then climbs back up a line of steep stone steps, full of interesting fossils, and follows rising ground with good views to Calling Low Farm. Beyond it, it crosses fields, passes through an area of woodland known as Low Wood, and returns to the road. A short distance away to the left is a long belt of trees, and right at its end is Bee Low, a large mound dating from the Bronze Age. Beneath it was found the bones of at least seven individuals, adults and children, buried in cists and rock-cut graves along with beakers and a number of bronze awls. Other cremation burials had also been inserted into the mound.

The walk crosses the road, takes the quiet lane opposite, and then turns off along the signposted path beside the car park. There are excellent views to Chatsworth House and the East Moors before the paths drops down to another lane which can be followed pleasantly back to Middleton.

This is a long walk, but as it circumnavigates Arbor Low, it serves to put the great monument in its true context, helping you to see the landscape as it must once have been. Hidden beneath the thin veneer of modern farmland, picture a land of scattered settlements in clearings within a thin woodland, falling away to a deep limestone gorge of secret caves and hidden rock shelters. Rising above it, on the crest of a high, rounded hill and standing beside the tomb of the ancestors, is the great stone temple of Arbor Low.

15. Wolfscote Hill
Biggin

Approx. distance: 8 miles

Approx. time: 4 hours

Starting point: Biggin GR 155594

Grade: A long but easy walk, with a steep pull up Wolfscote Hill

O.S. Maps: Explorer sheet OL 24; Landranger sheet 119

Grid references: Wolfscote Hill GR 137583; Nettly Knowe GR 152562; Liff's Low GR 154577

Just a few straggling rows of houses and a church, the village of Biggin sits high on the bleak limestone plateau of the White Peak, a little more than a mile from where the River Dove plunges into the deep dales for which it is so famous. Wolfscote Hill is just one of the line of hills which rise above the gorge, each capped in ancient times by a great stone tumulus.

When they were raised almost four thousand years ago, they must have looked spectacular. Built of blocks of white stone, they would have been clearly visible standing out against the sky. Even now, when the rock has weathered and the grass has slowly crept over them, and the degradation of time has reduced them to mere shadows of their former glory, they are still prominent features in the landscape.

Little is known of the secrets that most of them held, fortune hunters and historians in earlier times having plundered the remains that they once covered. Only one of them, known as Liff's Low, sitting on a high col between two of the hills, remained untouched long enough for its amazing treasures to be recorded and preserved. This walk weaves its way through this ancient landscape, climbing high into the hills, dropping deep into the dales, and visits this important site where all those years ago a great man was ceremoniously laid to rest.

When I last walked to Wolfscote Hill it was a sharp winter's day. A low sun in a blue sky cast long shadows over the frozen fields. Black crows sat hunched and silent on the fence posts, standing out clear against the backdrop of the snow-streaked hills.

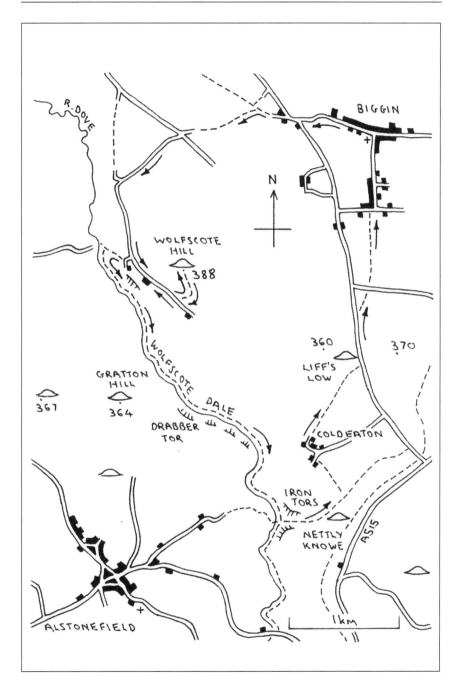

The walk begins along the lane which heads west out of the village, past Biggin Hall, and down the hill to where a farm track forks off to the left. The track, formed in parts by solid slabs of limestone, climbs up, forks left again and drops down to reach a tiny lane. Hartington Church tower can be seen ahead, above where the River Dove meanders through a valley which is still wide and shallow. The lane climbs up and around the steep slopes of Wolfscote Hill, and above the point where the river enters the narrow confines of Wolfscote Dale.

Before our walk follows it, it takes a detour to climb up to the summit of Wolfscote Hill. Passing Wolfscote Grange, but before reaching the remote house at The Whim, a gate gives access to a track which climbs up onto the shoulder of the hill. The summit is just a short way up the broad rocky ridge.

A band of low, limestone crags rings the small summit plateau, upon which sits the great stone tumulus. Now largely grassed over and sur-mounted by a modern trig point, it is still a spectacular monument, standing over two metres tall and about twenty-four paces across. Inside the mound was discovered a stone cist containing the skeletons of two children along with a food-vessel to accompany them to the afterlife.

Its position is unrivalled. Beyond the deep dale of the Dove, twisting away to the south, rise Gratton Hill and Narrowdale Hill, each capped with an ancient barrow. To the east the rolling hills of the White Peak stretch away into the distance.

It is a wonderful place to sit and an easy place to let the imagination recreate the landscape as it must once have been. Above the densely wooded valleys, the high hills must have risen clear to tops capped with the huge white tombs of the dead.

From the summit, the route is retraced to the lane and back past Wolfscote Grange to where a tiny lane turns down into the valley bottom, signposted for the isolated Rock Cottage. A good track takes you past the cottage and down into the dale bottom. Steep limestone crags rise above slopes of scree and scattered hawthorns which drop to the river lined with hazel trees.

On that last winter's day it was a delight to follow alongside the river. Icicles hung like bars along the banks and each stone standing above the water was capped with ice. Over the river, the trees hung, frosted white. Mallards swam in pairs, while solitary herons stalked the banks, and the vivid blue of a kingfisher skimmed low over the water.

Wolfscote Hill

It was very easy to imagine the dale as it would have been thousands of years ago as the Ice Age was drawing to a close. The first Stone Age hunters, travelling northwards, would have found shelter there from the arctic winds on the plateau above.

The track runs beside the river for some two miles, past the dramatic pinnacles of Drabber Tor, the open grassy slopes of Coldeaton Bank, past Biggin Dale and Gipsy Bank to the dense woodland below the Iron Tors. Here the route turns away to the left following the edge of the woodland up a narrow, cliff-lined side-valley. At the last of the trees, the path divides into three. The one to the right climbs up and over the hillside to the site of another, much denuded and reduced tumulus, known as Nettly Knowe. Instead, our route takes the path to the left, up the steep bank and across open fields to the very isolated little settlement of Coldeaton. Linked to the road by little more than a farm lane, this small group of farms and cottages sits up on the end of a high spur of land above the dale. The path joins the lane and follows it between the buildings and out onto the farmland beyond. Away to the left, Wolfscote Hill and its barrow can be clearly seen. The route takes a straight course over the fields, heading for the hilltop ahead, to join a quiet lane climbing up to a high col between it and the next hill.

Just a short way along the lane, in the field to the left, is Liff's Low. This great tumulus, now only a stony, misshapen mound sitting like an

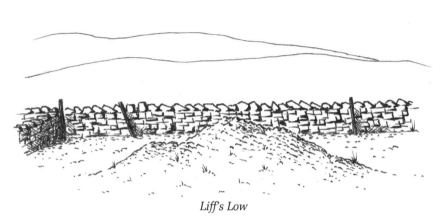

Liff's Low

island in the corner of the field, has given us one of the most important insights into the customs of the people who lived here some four thousand years ago.

Excavated initially by Thomas Bateman in 1843, and many times subsequently, the story it tells us is a fascinating one. The mound, which itself dates from the late Neolithic, is built upon the site of a much older structure. A hearth, a number of post holes, a scattering of worked stone and a pit containing charcoal dating from over a thousand years earlier, lies directly below the mound. Perhaps it is mere coincidence, or perhaps the place still retained some importance as an already ancient site when the tumulus was raised.

At the heart of the mound was an octagonal, limestone cist. Within it lay the intact skeleton of a man, lying on his side with his knees drawn up. By his knees was placed a hammer, skilfully crafted from the antler of a red deer. Behind his shoulders were placed two flint arrowheads, two flint chisels, two spearheads and two knives, one of which had a beautifully worked and serrated, saw edge. A pair of huge tusks from a wild boar was placed beside them and a small cup was placed over the tools. Several pieces of ochre were found beside it, that when wetted were still able to colour the skin a bright red.

Of greatest significance was the fact that this burial indicated an important change in culture from a communal identity for the ancestors, to one where individuals were seen as important, even in death. The addition of grave goods was a very early sign of a belief in an after-life as an individual. In the outer layers of the mound, Bateman also found evidence of later, additional burials, perhaps showing that, for some at least, this place remained as an important and significant site.

Reduced as it is by thousands of years of weather, farming and the activities of the many historians who have dug into it, Liff's Low remains a poignant and atmospheric site. Who was this man? Was he loved? Was he feared? What had he done to be honoured in such a way? It is easy to imagine a hunter, face splashed red with ochre, laid to rest in his great, stone sarcophagus, with the weapons and trophies of his life laid beside him. But of the man himself, only our imagination can fill in the details. In truth he was probably little different from those that stand and stare at the rough grassy mound that is all that remains today.

From Liff's Low, the lane is followed for just a short way to where a footpath turns off to the right, crosses fields, and another narrow lane to reach the first houses on the outskirts of Biggin.

This is a walk which is well worth doing for the scenery alone. Wolfscote Hill, with its wide, open views, contrasts sharply with the narrow world of the deep dale which runs beneath it. The historical remains are less tangible, mere shadows and suggestions of a time and a world that have long gone. But to visit them on a hard winter's day is a true delight, the stillness and the silence perhaps making those faint shadows of the past just a fraction less faint than under the bright sun of a busy summer.

16. Thor's Cave
Manifold Valley

Approx. distance: 6 miles

Approx. time: 4 hours

Starting point: Grindon GR 085545

Grade: A strenuous walk on quiet paths with magnificent views. Exploring Thor's Cave requires some easy scrambling, and permission is required to enter Dafar Ridge Cave

O.S. Maps: Explorer sheet OL 24; Landranger sheet 119

Grid references: Thor's Cave GR 098549; Thor's Fissure GR 098549; Elder Bush Cave GR 098548; Darfar Ridge Cave GR 098559; Ossum's Crag Cave GR 095557; Wettonmill rock shelters GR 095562

Nowadays the Manifold valley is a favourite haunt of tourists who wander along the old railway track beside the river and admire the occasional glimpse of towering cliffs rising above the wooded slopes. Few probably realise that these cliffs hold secrets which take us back to the very dawn of Man's colonisation of these northern hills at the end of the last Ice Age. For they are riddled with caves, some with wide gaping mouths visible for miles, others no more than narrow fissures hidden away beneath the dense undergrowth. Within them have been found, and still await to be found, clues to the area's fascinating history dating back for over ten thousand years.

When the first men arrived here, as the ice sheets retreated into the northern mountains, they would have found a bleak and harsh landscape of almost arctic tundra, inhabited by huge beasts such as mammoths and woolly rhinoceros. They would have come in the brief summer months, following the herds of reindeer and bison, finding temporary refuge in the caves and rock shelters of the Manifold Valley. They left little evidence of these fleeting visits, just the occasional flint blade or a scattering of charcoal in a simple hearth.

As the climate warmed and the land greened, the hunters and gatherers of the Mesolithic period became more settled within their own distinct territories. They would have lived in simple huts of wood and thatch, using the caves much as their forefathers had as places to take

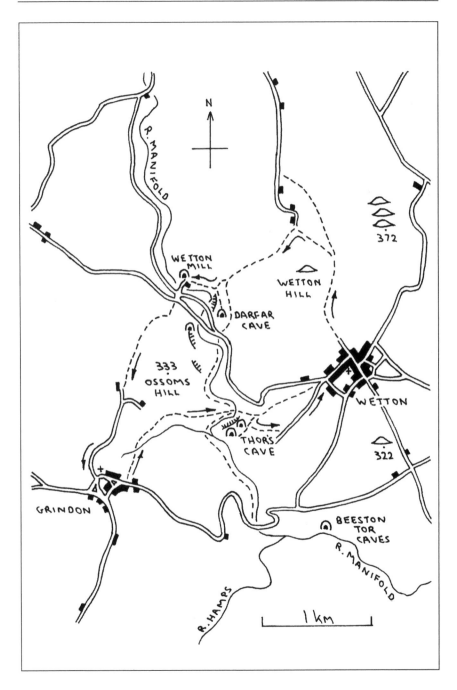

shelter in, to cook a meal in, or spend an occasional night between camps.

When the change to farming arrived, the caves took on a new significance. They came to be seen, not as shelters for the living, but of the dead. They became tombs, hidden away from the places where the people lived on the open slopes above the thickly wooded gorges. Bodies were placed, sometimes singly, sometimes in larger groups, along with a few treasured, tools and possessions. Pottery, perhaps containing the provisions they might need for an onward journey, was often placed beside them.

Although this type of burial had largely died out by the Iron Age, the caves continued to be visited and used right through the Roman Period and into Medieval times.

To visit this truly ancient landscape, our walk begins in Grindon, up on the limestone plateau above the deep defile of the Manifold Valley, and takes the lane running east, out of the village towards the valley. Before the last of the houses is reached, a footpath turns off to the left and drops steeply down into a side valley of the Manifold. The path is indistinct until it has crossed the small stream, where a good track leads along the upper fringe of the woodland in the valley bottom. The path passes below the isolated house at Ladyside and then plunges into the wood.

Little used and somewhat overgrown, it weaves through a dense growth of hawthorn, ash and hazel with the occasional sudden and dramatic view ahead to where the crags of Thor's Cave rise out of the forest. The cave itself and the much smaller Elder Bush Cave are clearly visible even from this distance.

The path then drops suddenly into the main valley, crosses over the popular track of the Manifold Way and the river, and begins to climb again along a well-paved track. After a short distance a path turns off to Thor's Cave, climbing steeply through the wonderfully coppiced hazel woods to reach the rocks below the yawning mouth of the cave.

A scramble is required to reach the inner sanctum but it is well worth the effort. High vaulted ceilings of water-smoothed minerals cascade down to strange, fluted, rock outcrops. The two huge entrances let in the wind as well as the light, but around the corner of one of several twisting passages is a large chamber completely sheltered from the outside elements.

Within the cave was found the body of a woman from the early

Thor's Cave

Bronze Age, together with a polished stone axe, pottery and bronze and amber jewellery. It is an awe-inspiring place on a scale unusual and unexpected in Britain.

From the cave entrance another path can be taken which climbs up and around the cliffs to the left to reach their rocky summit, and a viewpoint unrivalled in the Peak District.

The cliffs below are steep and dangerous, but it is possible to wander along their crest of the ridge to visit several other caves which can be found along the top of the escarpment. The first is a shallow cave with a twin-arched entrance and beyond it the larger entrance of Elder Bush Cave. Inside were found ancient hearths, burnt charcoal and bones which date back to over ten thousand years ago, along with flint tools and pottery which ranged from the Neolithic period right up to the time of the Romans.

Another cave known as Thor's Fissure is just a narrow slit in the rocks close to its much larger namesake, but within it were found Palaeolithic flints and six Neolithic burials along with a polished stone axe, pottery, jewellery along with the bones of several unusual creatures.

This is a marvellous area to explore, but it must always be remembered that there are many dangerous slopes and cliffs below and extreme caution is advised at all times.

From the back slope of Thor's Cave a well-marked footpath cuts across a sloping field to meet a farm track which can be followed into the village of Wetton, which sits on a col between the hills. From the centre of the village and close to the church, a lane leads out to the north signposted for the 'Back of Ecton'. It soon becomes a rough track leading to an old quarry, from where a footpath turns off onto lovely sheep pasture rising up towards Wetton Hill. The path runs between its two tops, each crowned with Bronze Age tumuli, where it forks, the left-hand path curling down and around the western hill towards several isolated houses in a narrow valley.

As the valley is entered, the stream, which normally flows down to this point, disappears down a 'swallow hole', leaving just a dry river bed downstream. Only after heavy rain will it burst into life again. Streams like this are known locally as 'rindles'. It is a lovely section of the walk down the valley, the steep grassy sides dotted with low hawthorn bushes and a few majestic ash trees. Just before the valley swings sharply round to the left, a footpath turn off to the right, and this is followed uphill to the top of a low ridge.

This is Darfar Ridge and it is well worth leaving the footpath at this point and wandering along its broad crest for a short way. Just as it begins to drop down, there is a metal grid covering an infill of rocks. This was an entrance to Darfar Ridge Cave. Although now blocked off, the cave can still be entered by a new entrance hidden away beneath the overhanging ash trees and elderberry bushes just off to the left of the ridge.

Within its narrow confines were found the bones of several of our Neolithic ancestors along with a leaf-shaped arrowhead, a several tiny flint tools. Beyond the outer chamber where the bones were discovered, the cave roof drops to a low creep before it opens again into a magnificent chamber richly decorated with mineral flows, gour pools (crystal pools formed by water dropping onto flow stone) and stalagmite pillars. How amazed must our ancestors have been when they first entered this strange, subterranean world?

To enter the cave, which is locked, permission and a key must be obtained from the South Peak Estate Office of the National Trust, tel. 01335 350503, but it is only advised for those experienced in caving techniques. For the rest, it is enough to sit outside the original entrance

Elder Bush Cave

and admire the magnificent view down the glorious Manifold Valley. Thor's Cave is directly ahead, Ossum's Crag Cave off to the right, and below, hidden among the wooded slopes are at least ten more caves which have been found to contain the remains of our distant ancestors. This truly is our very own, 'Valley of the Kings'.

The path from the ridge drops quickly down to Wetton Mill in the main valley. Just above the café are several very prominent rock shelters which can be easily reached from the path. They were used in Mesolithic times and later as a tomb for an adult and three young children. In fact, pottery and other artefacts show a continuity of use right up into post-medieval times.

From beside the small ford close to the café, a path climbs steeply up the slopes of Ossum's Hill, then turns sharply to the right around the hilltop. As it climbs, the view widens to take in the upper valley of the Manifold and the distant moors to the west. The shapely spire of Butterton Church rises above Butterton village with its well-known ford, and directly ahead, that of Grindon Church marks the way ahead. An isolated farm is soon reached from where a track leads to a quiet lane which can be followed pleasantly all the way back to the end of the walk.

This is a superb walk, visiting a busy and popular area but along paths which are little used. It climbs over high hills with wide views and drops into deep shadowy valleys cloaked in ancient woodland. It passes caves, within which has been found evidence of our earliest ancestors in northern Britain. Little changed for thousands of years, they are the perfect places to reach back into the past and touch a time now lost to us. It is not difficult to let the imagination free and picture the strange events which once took place within them. The bones, the tools and the pottery all tell us much about the people and their way of life, but other clues are less tangible and much harder to explain. None more so than in Thor's Fissure, where they found, beside the Neolithic burials and almost a hundred miles from the sea, several carefully placed bones from a dolphin!

17. Long Low
Wetton

Approx. distance: 7 miles

Approx. time: 3-4 hours

Starting point: Wetton GR 107552

Grade: A lovely walk in fine scenery, along well-marked and easy to follow footpaths

O.S. Maps: Explorer sheet OL 24; Landranger sheet 119

Grid references: Long Low GR 122539; Pea Low GR 131565

The village of Wetton sits in the limestone hills just above the steep gorge of the Manifold Valley. Its mellow stone cottages and farmhouses fit comfortably within this ancient landscape, and are very much a part of a pattern of settlement which dates back to the earliest times in our history. This walk visits two of the most significant, if sadly reduced, prehistoric monuments in the whole of the Peak District, and gives the visitor a chance to explore a landscape rich in clues to its Neolithic past.

The walk begins in the village itself, taking a quiet lane running from the main street out to the south-east. It climbs gently to where a low hill, just off to the right of the lane, is capped by a Bronze Age barrow. Beyond it the lane ends and the route follows a farm track up another rise into a landscape of open fields bordered with low limestone walls. A few scattered trees and the occasional stone barn are all that break the uncluttered skyline.

The track at this point follows a high promontory of land, falling away on either side into the deep, shadowy valleys of the Dove and the Manifold. Ahead, Long Low will be clearly visible now as an undulating ridge running along the crest of a long spur stretching off to the left of the track. A limestone wall runs along its uneven grassy crest, and at first glance it appears to be no more than a natural feature of the landscape.

On closer inspection, however, it becomes obvious that this is in fact, a huge man-made monument. Over 200 metres long, it is the only

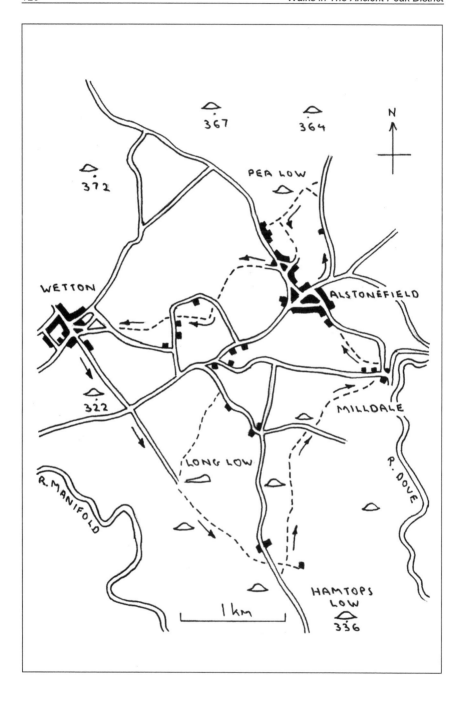

example in the Peak District of a bank barrow, and was originally built of rough limestone blocks piled over a central spine of vertical slabs set into the ground. At either end is a large round mound. It is likely that the structure evolved over a period of time and that its final shape was not how it was originally built. It almost certainly dates from the very early part of the Neolithic Period, and is therefore one of the oldest of the monuments in the area.

When it was excavated in the 19th century, a shallow forecourt was found at the north-eastern end. Inside was a chamber which held the bones of thirteen people piled up on a rough pavement of stones, along with the bones of oxen, pigs, deer and dogs. Further human remains were also found, interred along the length of the barrow.

Five thousand years ago this must have been an amazing sight, the white stone bank and mounds visible for miles, running along the sky-line of its high ridge. Sadly, over the intervening millennia, both natural and human actions have reduced this great monument to the hummocky grass ridge that we see today. Much stone has been taken to build the nearby walls, the forecourt and entrance have long gone and the stones have gradually slipped and slumped and been grassed over. The wall which follows its crest sits comfortably enough on the barrow, but this is more than can be said for the large metal water tank which has been placed on the top of the southerly mound.

Despite all these blemishes, Long Low remains an evocative site. Its position, high on its hilltop, still dominates the surrounding country-side, and it still has that air of timelessness that only the most special of ancient places have retained.

A footpath runs away below the barrow, dropping down to Hopedale, but our route continues on towards Damgate, passing the southerly mound on the left. Another round barrow sits in the first field to the right of the path, and in front, several more are clearly visible, including Hamtops Low on its prominent hilltop directly ahead.

The path skirts around a farmhouse to meet a quiet lane which is crossed, and a rising path taken in the direction of a stone barn. Before it is reached, the route drops down to the left and follows a line of stiles which lead through a shallow dry valley. It crosses fields which in the springtime are splashed with the bright yellow of dandelions growing in such abundance that they look like a commercial crop. Pale may-flowers stand up amongst them and celandines grow in the shadow of the stone walls, while up above skylarks sing incessantly.

Long Low

The well-marked path passes the head of a narrow side valley dropping down into Dovedale, and then climbs up to a narrow stone track. Just a short way along it, another path turns off beside a large earthen tumulus, now colonised by a large and very active sett of badgers, before dropping steeply down to Milldale. This is a popular beauty-spot and the crowds which flock here to sit beside the river and stand on its beautiful old bridge provide a sharp contrast with the quiet and empty landscape of the hills behind.

A tiny lane climbs up in the direction of Alstonefield, and this is followed for just a short way until a path leads up a very steep slope and over a pleasant field to arrive at the same destination. The church tower of Alstonefield stands out clearly to mark the way, while off to the left Long Low can still be made out on its now-distant hilltop.

The route takes you through the village, past its popular pub and its crowded green, and out along a farm track towards Gratton Hill. Within just a few moments you are back in a quiet and peaceful landscape of walled fields, wild flowers and only the sound of the birds to break the silence. The track passes a large barn; up ahead, Wolfscote Hills peers around the shoulder of Gratton Hill and away to the left Narrowdale Hill rises steeply to its cairn-topped summit. A path leaves the track and crosses one field in the direction of Narrowdale, but then turns left and follows the stone wall towards Pea Low which is now clearly visible up ahead.

This once-great chambered tomb is still a substantial monument, being well over forty paces across and four metres high, but like Long Low, it too has suffered from both the ravages of time and the thoughtlessness of antiquarians and landowners over the years. Three walls meet on its summit, and the scars of old excavations are very evident on its flanks, but it remains a prominent feature in the landscape.

It is mirrored by a tree-covered and natural, rocky mound only about a hundred metres away to the west, at the other end of the ridge of high ground on which it sits. Between the two are the remains of a small quarry topped with a stone wall, which is most likely the original source of the large quantities of stone which would have been needed to construct a monument of this size.

It is fascinating to picture the scene. Men, women and children working with antler picks, hacking away at the loose earth and rock to expose the slabs of white stone beneath. Large blocks, prized from this natural bedrock with wooden wedges and levers, being carried or dragged along the ridge to where they would be placed in ever-higher layers over the stone chamber at the heart of the tomb.

It must have been a considerable undertaking, and one that would have required a degree of organisation and cooperation from, what must have been, a sizeable community. It paints a picture of a complex society, with leaders and planners and people of vision. It tells us that they held strong beliefs and that they were a people prepared to work hard for a community that held its dead in great respect. I like to think that it was a labour of love, but perhaps that is no more than a modern sense of sentimentality for days gone by. Perhaps the workers had no real choice, and that they were compelled to work by a society that they felt no stake in. We shall probably never know!

What is certain is that the noise and bustle of those ancient days are long gone, and Pea Low now sits astride its ridge, largely forgotten by all but the few walkers who wander over its flanks and marvel at the strange hump in the landscape. Whenever I have been there I have seen no one and it is a perfect place to sit and let the imagination run free.

Pea Low

From the barrow the path continues, dropping down towards some large farm buildings on the outskirts of Alstonefield. Before they are reached, the path turns sharp left and leads after only a short distance to a lane which can be followed to the road where a number of pretty, stone cottages surround a small green. After crossing the road, another track leads into a shallow, dry valley which runs beneath a tree-capped hill called Steep Low. A large rookery sits in the tallest trees and the birds wheel and scream as you pass.

Another lane is crossed and the route continues along a path paved with stone slabs. After a hundred metres it turns right, over another lane, climbs a hill past a small square of sycamore trees, and on over the fields to the outskirts of Wetton.

This is a lovely walk by any standard, through scenery which typifies the limestone plateau of the White Peak. Evidence of prehistoric man's subtle fingerprint on the landscape is everywhere, and in Long Low you have an opportunity to visit one of the most forgotten, but significant monuments of the Neolithic Period in the whole of the north of England.

18. The Lows
Tissington

Approx. distance: 6 miles

Approx. time: 3-4 hours

Starting point: Tissington GR 177521

Grade: Pleasant walking over fields and rolling hills, along footpaths which are not always easy to follow

O.S. Maps: Explorer sheet OL 24; Landranger sheet 119

Grid references: Bose Low GR 169526; Sharp Low GR 161529; Stand Low GR 159536; Moat Low GR 155540; Bostern Grange Low GR 151534; standing stones GR 168523 and GR 169525

Tissington is an ancient settlement. The recorded history begins as a small Saxon village, and if you walk around it today the Norman church, the Civil War defences and the Jacobean Hall are all obvious signs of its long past. There are also the famous wells, which at Ascensiontide are dressed and which attract thousands of visitors each year. It is these that give us our first clues to a much longer past, which dates back to well before the invading Saxons first set foot in England.

From the very earliest of times natural springs had been seen as special places where people stopped as they travelled across the land. Then, as the hunters became farmers, they chose these places for their settlements. The springs, like caves, began to be seen as entrances to the 'mother earth', from which life-giving water emerged as a gift from the 'great goddess'. By the time the Romans first recorded the beliefs of the local Iron Age people, they were still worshipping the springs as the home of spirits, and our traditions of decorating wells and throwing coins into pools for luck date back to this time. With the coming of Christianity, these older Pagan traditions were not abandoned but simply incorporated into the new religion.

Tissington, with its light, easily farmed soils and natural supply of fresh water, would have been a perfect place to settle and has probably been lived in since the Neolithic period. One only has to look up to the surrounding hills, to the great tumuli that were built on their summits, to see that it must have been a centre of a great community. Known

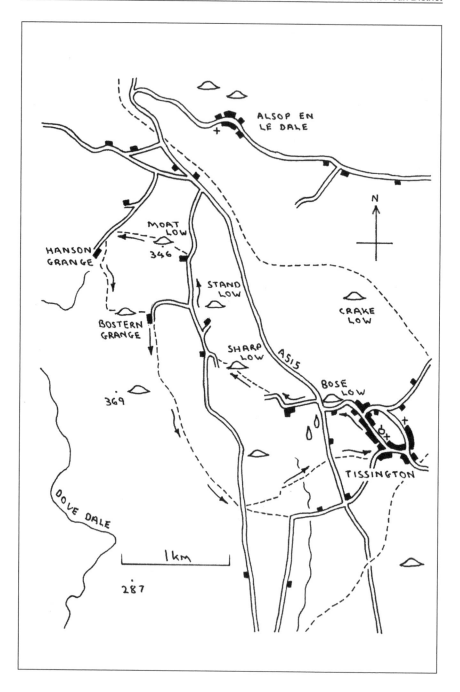

locally as 'Lows', these ancient, hilltop tombs lie largely forgotten and ignored by all but the few who venture into the quiet hills which rise above the village. This walk gives you the opportunity to do just that.

It begins in the village itself where the wells can be visited before setting off past the Hall and out along Rakes Lane. Just before you reach the main road, in a triangular walled enclosure to the right of the lane, is Bose Low, where the crouched skeleton of a 'very old man' was discovered.

This immense mound still stands a full five metres high, but is now so overgrown with brambles and thorn bushes that it is easily overlooked, and almost impossible to appreciate the prominence it must once have had in the landscape. It is only at the end of the walk that something will be discovered which shows just how important this burial site once was.

Crossing over the road, the route takes the driveway for Sharplow Farm, then follows the track past the farm and up the hillside beyond. As the slope eases off, it is possible to turn off the track and cross the open grassland towards a small copse of trees on the hilltop off to the right. There, beneath the sycamore trees and within a small, circular enclosure is Sharp Low. Although little more than a hummocky mound remains, just a few loose rocks showing now between the tree roots, it is still possible to imagine the tomb as it must once have been, clear of trees and rising above the Neolithic landscape.

Dropping down from the tumulus, the path briefly rejoins the farm track before it meets a high lane beside Gag Lane Barn. This lane is followed northwards, past Standlow Farm with its own tumulus on the small hill behind it, to Moat Low Farm. Above it on the hilltop is Moat Low itself.

This huge, flat-topped mound is still over two metres high and, although surmounted with a copse of beech trees, it still offers commanding views in all directions over the surrounding countryside. To the east the great chambered cairn of Minninglow can be seen on the horizon, while to the north the deep gorge of upper Dove Dale can be seen winding away into the distance. All around are more hills, each crowned with its own ancient cairn.

Within the mound was found a long, irregular grave, with two crouched skeletons accompanied by a bronze axe and the jaw of a pig!

From Moat Low, the path drops down to meet a lane running between the farmhouses of New Hanson Grange and Hanson Grange

Moat Low

itself. Turning towards the latter, the lane is followed up to its entrance where a path skirts around the farm buildings and the lovely old farmhouse and down into a narrow valley dropping steeply down into Dove Dale. The path up the valley is taken for only a short way before climbing the hillside to another small hilltop. Beneath the trees is yet another 'Low'. Much dug into and badly damaged, it is a sad reminder of the disrespect shown to some of these ancient tombs in more recent times.

Below the mound is Bostern Grange Farm, and the path drops down and around it, passing through the farmyard before breaking out onto the fields beyond. It contours around the side of a hill and climbs gently up to a high col. Away to the right on the near skyline are the remains of yet another tumulus. Ahead, the view out across the lower Dove Valley to the Midlands is fascinating. From this southerly outpost of the Peak District hills, the lowlands stretch away into the hazy distance, only the cooling towers of the old coalfields raising their heads above the level landscape.

From this high point, the path drops steadily down, over high fields, passing an old quarry and limekiln until it eventually reaches a track which leads down to a narrow lane. Beyond the lane are two footpaths, our route takes the left-hand, and higher, path which climbs up briefly before dropping steeply down into the valley of the Wash Brook. The fields in this valley are mostly grazing land now, but still contain some of the best preserved examples of ridge and furrow that I have ever seen. The path generally runs along the crests of the ridges, only occasionally dipping down into a furrow before following the next.

The stream is crossed over a small stone bridge and from there the path climbs again towards the main road which runs along the top of the hillside ahead.

The first time I crossed over this bridge, I had stopped in the field just beyond it to watch a flock of long-tailed tits moving relentlessly along the lines of hazel trees lining the stream. When I turned back, I noticed that I could see Bose Low up on the skyline off to the left. Then I spotted two large stones standing in the field between myself and the tumulus. They appeared to be standing upright and were perfectly aligned with it.

Standing stone aligned with Bose Low

Not marked on any maps as standing stones, nor mentioned in any reference that I have, these stones appear to be ancient stones aligned with the great tumulus on the hilltop. The nearest stands about four feet high, and the second is somewhat taller. Both are of extremely weathered limestone and must have been exposed to the elements for centuries. They are certainly not recently quarried stones. The ridges and furrows of the field also appear to work around the stones, suggesting that they pre-date this early form of farming. Neither of the stones appears to be lying naturally, and, although the first stone is a rough shapeless block, it has certainly been stood on end. The further of the two stones, and the one nearer to the tumulus, is more shapely and definitely stands upright. It is so weathered that, in places, the hollows go completely through the stone. This is common with many ancient standing stones.

If they are indeed ancient stones, what were they? Perhaps they are all that remains of other stones which once circled the mound. Such complexes are known in both Wales and Scotland and as far away as Brittany, but would be unusual for the Peak District. Perhaps they formed part of an avenue of stones which once led towards the place of burial. Again, such structures are not known locally, but are found in other areas of the country. If either of these possibilities is correct, it looks likely that the overgrown and now almost totally disregarded mound of Bose Low was, and therefore still is, a site of much greater significance than its present sad and sorry condition deserves.

From the field in which the stones stand, a footpath climbs up to the main road and crosses over it. It then continues downhill to meet a beautiful avenue of lime trees which can be followed back into Tissington and the end of the walk.

19. Carsington Pasture Brassington

Approx. distance: 7 miles

Approx. time: 4 hours

Starting point: Brassington GR 231544

Grade: An interesting walk along little-used paths, but the pleasant scenery is somewhat spoiled by the many quarries and works which still operate in this area.

O.S. Maps: Explorer sheet OL 24, Landranger sheet 119

Grid references: Carsington Pasture cave GR 242536; Wirksworth standing stone GR 273543; Ivet Low GR 259544; Harborough Rocks GR 243553

Brassington is a delightful village of mellow stone cottages tucked away in a fold of the hills above the wide expanse of Carsington Water. Above the village is the high limestone plateau of Carsington Pasture. Now prized as a source of limestone, these hills were once the home to our Neolithic ancestors who farmed on their light soils. Almost five thousand years later, there are still clues to be found that tell us about these ancient people.

The walk begins in the village, from where a footpath climbs steeply up onto a southerly spur of the plateau. Enclosed fields soon give way to open grazing land studded with rocky outcrops and scattered hawthorns. From the top of the spur the path drops into a lovely secluded valley ringed with broken crags and tottering pinnacles.

It then rises to a col on the far side. Off to the right of the public footpath, on the crest of the slope looking south over Carsington Water, on the edge of an area of old mine workings, is a small cove of rocks. Inside it, at the bottom of an overgrown hollow, is a low entrance to a cave diving down beneath the rocks. It is almost impossible to enter now, and was probably very little different in Neolithic times.

Within it were placed the bones of nine adults and eleven children. Some of the bones showed signs of cut marks suggesting that they might have been de-fleshed before being placed within the tomb. With the human remains was a perforated bone pin, a carved antler and some Neolithic pottery. Of equal interest is the presence of Iron Age and

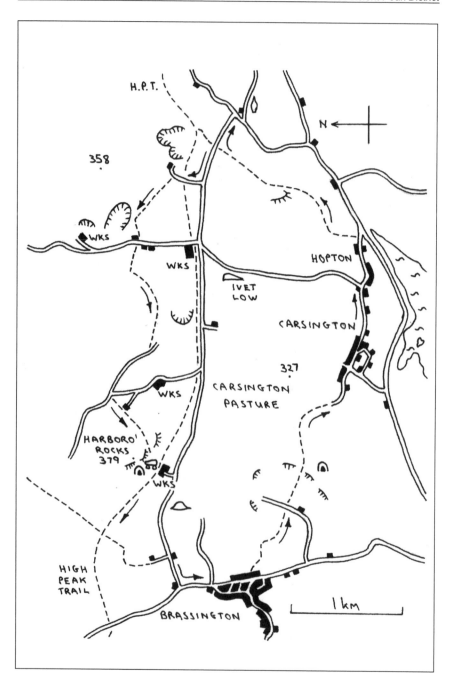

Roman artefacts which suggest that the cave was still known thousands of years after its initial use. This cave has only recently been rediscovered, suggesting that there could well be other similar tombs still hidden within the limestone hills of Derbyshire.

From the col, the path curls away to the left, dropping down across the hillside to join a good track leading easily down towards the village of Carsington itself.

Sitting on the springline, on a shelf above the valley floor and below the high pasture, it is typical of many of our current settlements in that it is probably on the same site that was chosen by the very first settlers in the area. The village has an old church and a Saxon cross, but it is quite possible that it was first lived in over three thousand years before either of these was raised. It merges into the next village of Hopton, with its old hall and strange ice house, and the route passes through both villages to where a footpath turns off to the left just before the lane joins the main road.

The path climbs up and across the hillside, passing above an area of woodland, to pleasant open grazing land. The humps and hollows of old mine workings are still very obvious as the path climbs again, around the side of a small crag and across the hillside to meet another lane. Away to the right below the path can be seen an isolated standing stone standing in a field beyond the main road at the bottom of the slope.

To reach the stone it is necessary to follow the lane for a short way, crossing over the main road to where it sits in a hay meadow. This is one of the few remaining standing stones to be found in the whole area, and is an impressive limestone blade. Over seven feet tall and five broad, it now leans slightly and is split down the middle, its broad sides decorated with fossilised limpet shells. Quite why it was raised here is now impossible to tell, although its broadest side leans back and faces up the hillside in exactly the direction of Ivet Low, an ancient long barrow on the crest of the ridge just out of sight to the west. Perhaps it was one of a line of waymarkers lining a route from the Derwent Valley up onto the high plateau of Carsington Pasture.

To return from the stone, retrace your steps back up the lane to where a farm lane leads off to the right. This crosses over the High Peak Trail which runs in a deep cutting below, and leads towards a group of farm buildings tucked into a rising hillside. Before they are reached, a footpath is taken which rises slightly before dropping down beside an old quarry to reach another road.

Wirksworth standing stone

The path crosses over and climbs up and around the next hill to reach a dirt lane running up to the high crest. Ahead, the pinnacles of Harborough Rocks can now be seen on the near skyline. The lane is followed as it drops down into a shallow valley, below a large industrial works and on to where the lane for New Harborough Farm turns off. Instead of taking the drive which winds across the hillside, take a footpath which heads directly for the farm, before skirting around it to the right. It then climbs back up onto open heathland and on towards the trig point which marks the high point of the Rocks.

Harborough Rocks are a succession of limestone tiers, one above the other, facing out to the south and west and rising to a high rocky summit. Evidence in the form of stone tools has been found here that suggests that this area was regularly visited by people as far back as the Mesolithic period. In the lowest tier of rocks is a large cave, which was undoubtedly used as shelter in these early times, but it was not until the Neolithic period that it came into use as a tomb. Perhaps a surviving social memory had already marked the site as a significant place, suitable as a repository for the bones of the ancestors.

The cave is easily found, and is now primarily used as a rain shelter

Harborough Cave

for the many rock climbers who flock to the crags. Inside is a large square chamber, open to the sky at one point where a narrow rock chimney splits the roof. At the back of the cave is a very low and narrow passage leading further into the hillside. Inside the cave were found the remains of at least two bodies along with Neolithic pottery, flint and chert tools, arrowheads and a Bronze Age beaker.

Not far from the cave, and almost certainly built there because of the proximity of the natural tomb, are the remains of a burial chamber. Part of the chamber remains, built into the naturally outcropping rocks, and the builders have used a natural fissure between the rocks as an entrance tunnel. The covering cairn has almost gone, but it is interesting to see how it blends into the natural features of the landscape to such an extent that it is difficult to tell what is natural and what man-made. Within the chamber and entrance passage were found the disarticulated remains of a number of individuals, along with broken pottery, flint tools and arrowheads.

Why two tombs so close together, containing similar material from a similar period? Perhaps one took the place of the other, or perhaps each served a different section of the community.

The site is a fascinating place, almost alive with the shadows of the past, but unfortunately spoilt somewhat by a large industrial plant just below the outcrops, which blights the view and adds a continuous background noise which is very difficult to ignore.

From the rocks a short path leads down to the High Peak Trail which runs between the Rocks and the factory. The trail is followed westwards and looking back, it gives good views of the tiers of rock rising up to the trig point. The trail follows a disused railway line and the industrial archaeology is interesting. It gives easy walking with good views but can be somewhat monotonous, although dodging the many cyclists which speed along it keeps the mind active. As it bends around the first corner, another path turns off and this is followed up the hillside to the left. The surrounding countryside is dotted with strange outcrops of limestone but the top of this small hill is quite extraordinary. It is a sheet of limestone pavement that has been exposed and is so weathered that the individual blocks are isolated and have been carved in places into tottering towers and spires.

The path crosses the hilltop and drops to a farm track which leads to the road. This is then followed easily back into Brassington.

This walk is different from most in this book, in that it isn't always amongst the pristine landscapes which we tend to associate with the Peak District. Pretty in parts and still largely agricultural, there is, none the less, a constant reminder of the recent industrial history of the area. In years to come this will probably be as fascinating as the more ancient archaeology which this walk seeks out. It does however serve to remind us that Carsington Pasture is, and has been for many thousands of years, a place where people live and work. Perhaps the people entombed in the caves would be glad to see that their landscape is still a vibrant and productive place.

20. Wigber Low
Bradbourne

Approx. distance: 4 miles

Approx. time: 2-3 hours

Starting point: Bradbourne GR 207526

Grade: A short but tricky walk following little used footpaths and farm tracks

O.S. Maps: Explorer sheet OL 24; Landranger sheet 119

Grid references: Bradbourne Church and carved stone GR 207526; Wigber Low GR 204514

The quiet village of Bradbourne sits on its low hilltop above the deep, wooded Havenhill Dale much as it has done for thousands of years. An old hall and a cluster of stone cottages huddle around an early Norman church on a quiet lane far removed from the hectic tourism of the National Park just a mile away to the west. It is perhaps best to start this walk in the churchyard, for it is there that the first clue can be found to the fascinating history of this truly ancient settlement.

Old as the church is, it stands on the site of a much older place of worship. An earlier Anglo-Saxon church stood there, and before that there was a stone which amazingly still stands in the churchyard. Originally in three pieces, this ancient stone now lacks its top section which is carved in the form of a cross, and has only recently been returned to the village. It is currently inside the church. The two central pieces were retrieved from the churchyard wall and remounted on a low base.

It is thought that it was originally painted in bright colours and would have been the centre of religious ceremonies before the first church was built. Two sides of the stone are carved in early Christian style with human figures, but it is the other two sides which are the most fascinating. Onto these are cut the strange spirals and concentric circles of a much more ancient pagan culture. Found throughout western Britain, these symbols are more usually associated with the standing stones and burial chambers of the Neolithic period.

Why then this strange mixture of symbolism? It is just possible that

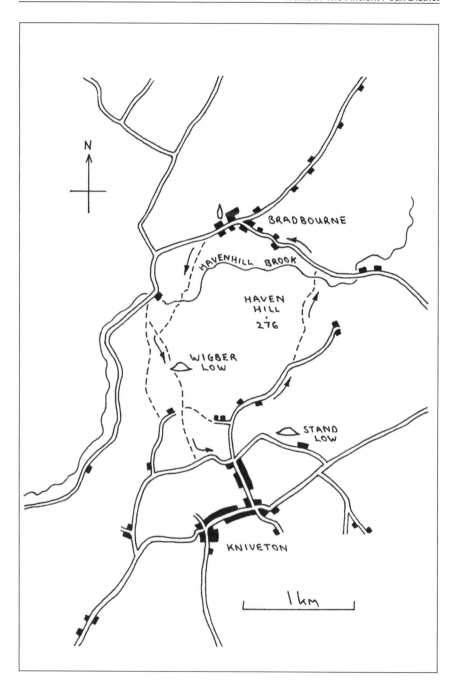

this is a much older stone marking a place of ancient importance that was re-carved and Christianised in more recent times. More likely is that it was indeed carved by early Christians, but at a time when elements of a much older pagan society still held out in this quiet backwater, and that the stone represents a people 'hedging its bets' and still adjusting to the new religion.

In support of the theory that the stone marks a site of very ancient significance, is the view to the south from the church. Haven Hill rises broad and squat in the foreground, but just peering around its sloping shoulder is the flat-topped crest of Wigber Low, the object of this walk and another clue to the mystery of the carved stone.

The walk begins along the quiet lane leading westwards from the church. Not far beyond the last of the houses a footpath turns off to the left and drops down across fields towards the thickly wooded Havenhill Dale. Just beyond a gate above the brook, the path turns unexpectedly to the right through a thick hedgerow and drops down to where two wooden footbridges take you to the far bank. Ignore the obvious farm track and instead follow along the stream for just a short way to where a stile marks the correct path, which climbs up the rather wild and overgrown hillside to join the main bridleway leading up to Wigber Low.

Still showing little evidence of heavy use, the path passes through an avenue of old hawthorns before breaking out into open fields just below the broken crest of the hill. There, on the very top, is a large oval platform of grey limestone. A ring of larger stones form a kerb around the perimeter of the cairn which runs for seventeen paces along the level crest of the ridge and is thirteen paces across, dropping away slightly to either side with the natural slope of the ground.

Despite its magnificent position, the cairn itself is unspectacular in appearance, and it was only when it was excavated that its remarkable history was revealed.

Over five thousand years ago this spot was chosen as place where the spirits of the dead could be released from their earthly bodies. Perhaps it was chosen because it was already a place of importance, although unmarked by any structure that remains today. It may well have been somewhere, above the thickly wooded valleys, where the hunters of earlier periods would have met with other groups, or set up seasonal camps.

A platform was built, onto which the dead were laid, to be consumed by the birds and beasts and the elements. This practice, known as excarnation, is a very ancient custom and it is thought that the bones, once clean and bleached by the weather, were removed to be used in ceremonies and possibly interred elsewhere. The evidence for this being such a platform, was a large number of small bones found between the stones, left when the larger bones were removed.

Eventually this practice must have died out because some thousand years later, the platform had become a place of more usual burials and a low mound of stones was raised over it. It then seemed to have remained unused for a long period, although still probably remembered as a place where the ancestors dwelt, for by the time of the Roman conquest, coins and tokens of respect

Carved stone in Bradbourne Churchyard

were still being placed within the cairn.

It is in the period that followed the Romans that the link with the settlement below the hill was once again restored. The local British population was overrun by incomers from across the sea, the Angles and the Saxons, who spread to most of England supplanting or at least subjugating the indigenous people of the area. Initially pagan, these new settlers came from a culture where burials in barrows was also a part of their history and perhaps because of this, the ancient cairn on the hill began to be used once more.

At least five new burials date from this time. A man and a woman lay side by side in one grave, while in another a woman and a young child. These burials included many grave goods, patterned swords, spears

Wigber Low

and amber jewellery from the Baltic, which suggested that these were people of some standing. Perhaps they were simply continuing a long-remembered tradition, or staking their claim to their new land, or perhaps they had become integrated with a remnant local population, for whom the hilltop was still seen as a mystical place.

It was also from this time that the great stone in the settlement below was being worshipped. Painted in bright colours and carved with spirals and circles, it may have been a focal point of a culture that looked once more on the distant hilltop with reverence. Then, as the old ways were replaced by a new religion, the stone was turned into a powerful Christian symbol and the first church built beside it. The people turned their back on Wigber Low which became a place to be shunned, a place where the evil spirits lurked.

Today it is a wonderful place to sit, to look out to distant Dovedale, marked by the easily identified Thorpe Cloud, or away to where the equally ancient burial chambers of Minningslow crown their own hilltop.

There are several footpaths down from Wigber Low. The most straightforward is to return to the track which runs just below the crest of the ridge, and to follow the line of stiles which drop slowly down and skirt around an isolated farm to join a quiet lane on the outskirts of

Kniverton. This can be followed eastwards to where another lane turns off in the direction of Newhouse farm. These lanes are bordered by wild hedgerows which in late summer are a tangle of brambles and splashed with the delicate pink of willowherb and foxglove, and in the occasional break in the hedge, Wigber Low stands out clearly, the prominent feature of the landscape.

The lane passes the farm and climbs up onto a high shoulder of Haven Hill, from where a track turns off, to drop down the far side. It enters a dry valley dotted with scattered hawthorns, which runs down into the main valley of Havenhill Dale Brook. This is crossed to meet the road leading quickly back to Bradbourne.

This short walk tells the story of a very ancient settlement, one that for thousands of years looked up to the hill of Wigber Low as the place from where their ancestors watched over them, giving them a sense of belonging, of being tied to their land. Through changing cultures, religions and political allegiances, it has been a part of the cement that held their community together. To this day the locals know of it by name as well as by sight, talk of it as a strangely 'cold' place, but are none the less happy to have it as a part of their history, a part of what still makes their community what it is today.

21. Weaver Hills
Wootton

Approx. distance: 4 miles

Approx. time: 2-3 hours

Starting point: Wootton GR 106452

Grade: A short walk, along well-marked but little-used footpaths, over gentle hills

O.S. Maps: Explorer sheet 259; Landranger sheet 119

Grid references: Weaver Hills barrows GR 097464 and GR 102462; Over Low GR 115462

The Weaver Hills form the very southerly edge of the high limestone plateau which we know as the White Peak. Below them the tiny villages of Wootton and Stanton sit on beds of gritstone that drop away into the valleys of the Churnet and the Dove. Although the western edges of the hills have been eaten into by quarrying over the last century, they remain as a quiet and peaceful haven on the fringe of the busy National Park.

Along the high crests and spurs of these hills are a number of ancient barrows, some in clusters and others standing in isolation, each still a prominent feature in the landscape.

To visit them, our walk begins in Wootton, a pleasant village of old stone houses with a tiny stream which runs down the side of the main street. Taking the road out to the west, a track soon turns off to the right in the direction of Wootton Cricket Club. After passing the club house, a footpath turns off the track and runs parallel to it, across fields, rising gradually up towards the foot of the hills.

Once over a last stile, the path rises across the open hillside, and it is immediately noticeable that the geology beneath the ground has suddenly changed. The heavy, deep soils of the gritstone are left behind, and are replaced by the dry, stony grasslands of the limestone. In places there are rocky outcrops, and only the occasional hawthorn tree raises itself above the sheep-cropped turf.

The path climbs over several terraces on the hillside, although

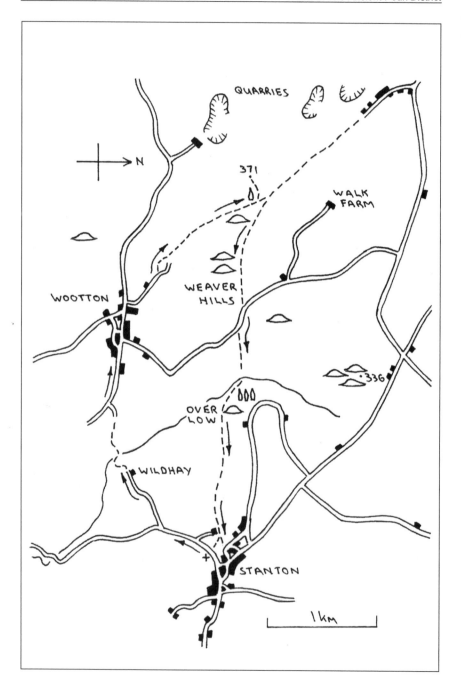

whether they are natural features of the landscape or the remains of ancient field systems isn't certain. A large badgers' sett in one of them would suggest a man-made earth structure rather than a natural rock feature, and it is highly likely that our ancestors would have used these high, southerly-facing slopes to farm on.

Climbing up towards the prominent trig point which marks the highest point of the Weaver Hills, a high col is reached. Just to the left of the path, in a drystone wall, is a pair of gateposts. One of them is of gritstone and stands out quite noticeably from the white limestone of the wall. It is also much more weathered than its partner and it is possible that this is in fact an ancient stone marking the col, which has since been utilised as a gatepost when the wall was built.

A stile and a short path take you quickly up to the top, which offers wide views out over the wooded Staffordshire hills and over the quarries which constantly nibble away at the western fringe of the hills.

Turning back, you can now look along the length of the escarpment, and the line of barrows running along the crest of the ridge. The first one sits astride the broad ridge, is about twenty paces across and still stands some two metres high. Where the surface grass has been disturbed you can get a good idea of its construction which appears to be a typical one of alternative layers of loose stone and earth. Several large hollows near to the barrow could well be the stone quarries where the rock was dug from.

The public footpath veers of to the left at this point, but it is possible to follow along the edge of the ridge towards another group of barrows several hundred metres further on. The first of these is even larger, being over twenty-five paces across and over three metres high. Its centre has been hollowed out and in the stony crater grows a wizened old hawthorn tree. A third barrow marked on the map appears as no more than a slight hump beside a sunken water tank, but the fourth is similar in size to the first two.

These typical Bronze Age barrows were probably raised over single burials, possibly in a rock cut grave or stone cist. The body would have been laid in a crouched position and might have been accompanied by jewellery or weapons to accompany them to the afterlife. These individual burials marked a significant change in culture from the communal burials of earlier times. In many cases however, other bodies or cremations were added at a later date and this would suggest that the idea of a community of ancestors was not completely dead.

Tumulus on the Weaver Hills

The positioning of the barrows is also typical, placed where they could be seen from a long way away. Interestingly, these are largely unseen from the villages directly below to the south, suggesting perhaps that the people who raised them lived on the more gentle slopes to the north. It has also been suggested that they also served the purpose of marking territory and were placed to be visible to rival communities many miles away.

At least seven more barrows can still be traced around the eastern and northern slopes of these hills, some of which can just be seen away off to the left of the path beyond Weaver Farm.

From the fourth barrow the path can be rejoined as it drops quickly down to meet a tiny lane climbing up to the farm. Turning right along the lane for about two hundred metres you will reach a footpath leading off to the left which drops down over fields. It contours around a high spur of land and down towards a wooded valley below.

It soon reaches a circular copse of hazel trees, which sit in a damp hollow beside a tiny stream. When I last passed, it was full of long-tailed tits flitting tirelessly from bush to bush, their tinkling song magical in the still air. High above the trees a lone buzzard wheeled silently away towards the distant hills.

The path skirts around the copse to the left and crosses the stream over a very narrow and slippery wooden bridge. At this point the geology changes again, passing back onto the gritstone. Gone are the dry, limestone walls and in their place are some of the strangest field bound-

Alignment of stones near Over Low

aries that I know. Large gritstone slabs stand vertically, like alignments
of standing stones. Between them smaller stones fill the gaps. In places
six or seven stones stand close together, and there are a number of these
lines around the edge of the first field. From their number, it must be
assumed that these are not truly ancient stones, but they appear to be
well-weathered and of some antiquity, and they are certainly most
unusual.

The path runs parallel to the stream and in the second field is the
large tumuli known as Over Low. Standing on a low bluff above the
stream this huge mound is still over forty paces across although its
height has been sadly reduced by centuries of farming. Judging from its
size, and its more low-lying position, it is possible that this is a much
older tomb than those crowning the crest of the hills up above.

From the mound the path turns away from the stream across fields,
following a line of stiles, each of which necessitates a tight squeeze
between two vertical stones, to pass from one field to the next. At times
difficult to spot, the stiles can be more easily located by heading for the
bell tower of Stanton Church which can just be seen, low on the horizon, up ahead.

As the path approaches the village it passes just to the left of a stone
house. Close by the house is an old oak tree, the trunk of which has
rotted so completely that it is possible to walk right through it. Here the
path forks, the route to the left climbing up to the village itself, which
can be explored, or the one to the right dropping down directly towards

the church. Either way works, the return route taking the lane past the church in the direction of Ellastone. This is followed for about four hundred metres until a farm lane turns off to the right leading to the remote farmyard of Wildhay. Here the lane becomes a rough track which drops into a wooded valley before climbing again and crossing fields to reach a lane on the outskirts of Wootton and the end of the walk.

About three miles to the south of the Wootton is that great icon of the modern age, the theme park of Alton Towers. It is fascinating to look up from the winding queues to the distant ridge of the Weaver Hills and to see on their high crest a line of ancient barrows rising from the skyline. In their time, they were probably just as symbolic and just as awe inspiring. But up there, time seems to have stopped, the ancestors still watch over the landscape now as they have done for almost four thousand years. How privileged we are to be able to visit still, the great monuments of our forefathers.

Western Moors

Castle Cliff Rocks

22. Lud's Church
Wincle

Approx. distance: 6 miles

Approx. time: 3-4 hours

Starting point: Danebridge GR 965653

Grade: A lovely walk along well marked paths, over high hills with stunning views

O.S. Maps: Explorer Sheet OL 24; Landranger sheet 118

Grid references: Hanging Stone GR 974654; Lud's Church GR 987656; Castle Cliff Rocks GR 986657; standing stone GR 970653

The River Dane flows through a deep and narrow valley as it drops down from the high moors of the Peak District onto the level plain of Cheshire. The valley curls around the base of a long ridge rising up to the broken crags of the Roaches. Hidden away in a secluded forest on the far slopes of the ridge, is a strange and mystical place known as Lud's Church.

This natural chasm, caused by a huge primeval landslip in the gritstone, is over fifty feet deep and barely six feet wide in parts, and runs like a jagged tear across the hillside. The vertical walls are surmounted by a luxuriant growth of ferns and moss, and stunted trees clinging precariously to the bare rock.

As its name suggests, this was a place of ancient pagan worship which most likely goes back to the very earliest times of human occupation in the area. The first visitors would have recognised it as a significant feature in the landscape, and successive generations would have come to think of it as somewhere special. As its name implies, it was still a place of worship in historic times and even today, in small niches in its rocky walls, can be found small tokens and the stumps of candles lit by people who still recognise it as a place apart.

The walk to find Lud's Church begins in Wincle, a scattered village on the steep slopes above the bridge crossing the River Dane. Below the bridge the tumbling waters of the river run whisky-brown between rocks, soft and green with moss. The lane climbs up to a lodge house

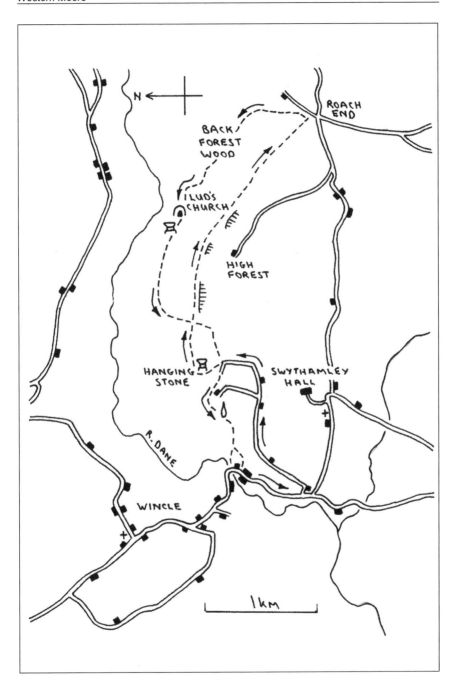

leading into the estate of Swythamley Hall, from where a lane climbs up and around the hillside towards Hanging Stone Farm. As it climbs, the views broaden and the shapely summit of Shutlingsloe appears ahead, while rising away to the right is a long curling ridge on which the dramatic rock formation of the Hanging Stone is immediately obvious.

To the right of the lane, over the high stone wall is a Bronze Age tumulus within the parkland of the Swythamley estate. The lane passes several houses before it abuts against the hillside and peters out into a rough track. Above and to the left is the Hanging Stone, its great rocky prow jutting out into the sky. A path climbs to it through the ferns, and steps curl around it to where a short scramble gives easy access to its top with its magnificent views back out over the Cheshire plain. It is almost certain that an ancient trackway passed close by here, leading from the Mersey Valley, past the Cloud and the Bridestones, before climbing up and over the ridge and on into the Peak District. The Hanging Stone must have been a notable feature and waymarker on the route.

Below its great overhang are two more recent memorial plaques, one to a Squire of Swythamley Hall killed in action in the Second World War, and another to an earlier squire's noble mastiff, Burke.

From the stone the path follows the ridge, initially through grazing land then over a bridleway onto the open moor of the High Forest. In late summer sunshine the contrasting colours of the mottled greens of the ferns and the deep purple of the heather create a stunning canvas of the walk ahead. The path rises and the right-hand side of the ridge breaks into broken crags, each, like the Hanging Stone, capped with an overhanging slab. It is a silent place, only the sound of the wind and the occasional whirr of grouse breaking the peace.

Ahead is the serrated edge of the Roaches and beyond them, Hen Cloud, with the glittering silver ribbon of Tittesworth Reservoir in the distance. Down to the left is the valley of the Black Brook which joins the Dane below the High Forest.

The ridge drops briefly then climbs gain to Roach End, where an unfenced lane crosses the hill. A path turns off to the left dropping down into the secluded woodland of the Back Forest Wood. This is a magical place, clinging to the steep hillside, and a line of stone steps leads down beneath its shadowy canopy. Many paths lead through the wood, but Lud's Church is well signposted as the route winds pleasantly between stunted oaks and tall pines on a track paved with interwoven tree roots.

Lud's Church

Lud's Church appears at first as no more than a few steps dipping down beneath the dense foliage, but they dive down into a deep dell overhung with trees and ferns. The chasm winds and splits, plunging deeper below the land surface above, between vertical walls split with chimneys and cracks. Towers and turrets of rock reach up to a narrow strip of sky. It is little wonder that it was seen as a special, and indeed sacred, site. At the far end another set of rough steps rise back to ground level, still overhung with a dense canopy of foliage, the green light adding to the mysterious nature of the place.

Lud's Church has been never been properly studied and little is known about its true history, but there is no doubt that it was, and is, a significant feature in the landscape and has been recognised as such for many thousands of years. Its link with ancient pagan beliefs is also

Standing stone below the Hanging Stone

something which has continued into recent times. A carved figurehead, known as Lady Lud, once stood high on the cliffs but was sadly destroyed only a few years ago.

A good track runs past the exit from the chasm, and our way turns to the left, winding through the thinning trees to reach another notable natural feature of the area, Castle Cliff Rocks. Here, whatever forces of nature split apart the land to create Lud's Church also made this confused jumble of rocky towers and deep shadowy fissures.

The route passes the rocks and the woodland peters out into an area of bilberry and scattered birch and rowan as it contours around the hillside in a deep and time-worn track. It is not beyond the bounds of possibility that this is the very path used for thousands of years as it passed through these hills on its way into the Peak. As it gradually rises, the views widen out and the strangely oppressive feel of the wood is dispelled as Shutlingsloe climbs once more over the near horizon.

The path soon reaches the dip in the main ridge passed earlier in the day, but then drops quickly down the far side to join a farm track running along the base of the hills. It passes beneath the Hanging Stone once more, and above the farm of the same name, to where a footpath turns off to the left across fields. In the second field, and close to the farm, is a standing stone. Almost as broad as it is high, this stone is in a perfect alignment between the Hanging Stone and the great burial chamber of the Bridestones on the slopes of the distant Cloud. Perhaps it was a waymarker on the ancient trackway which passed between them. Another clue to its possible siting lies just beyond it, where a natural spring, now controlled and piped, once bubbled from the ground.

The path skirts around the spring, and drops into a steep, wooded dell that drops down to join the River Dane in the main valley below. Within the wood the path splits and our route turns to the left, climbs briefly and then returns to the road along a lovely narrow path that winds down between the well-kept gardens of the village.

This is a marvellous walk, through scenery which typifies the best of the high gritstone edges of the Peak District. The views are wide and wonderful and the natural features both strange and spectacular. But above all these things is the sense of a timeless landscape, little changed for thousands of years. Our Neolithic ancestors might still be able to follow the track they once used and recognise the many features that it passes on its way. Perhaps they would be more amazed that somebody, on occasions, still lights a candle in the tiny niche within the deep chasm of the Back Forest.

23. Castle Naze
Combs

Approx. distance: 6 miles

Approx. time: 3-4 hours

Starting point: Combs GR 042786

Grade: A short but strenuous walk through beautiful, wild country

O.S. Maps: Explorer sheet OL 24; Landranger sheet 119

Grid references: Lady Low GR 065783; Cow Low GR 065786; Castle Naze Hillfort GR 054784

Combs is a tiny settlement close to, but remote from, the industrial towns of Whaley Bridge and Chapel-en-le-Frith. Tucked away in the narrow mouth of the deep Combs Valley it is ringed on all sides by high hills. Just a short way to the east and almost leaning over the village is the great rocky spur of Castle Naze. This spectacular crag-encircled promontory is the northern-most bastion of a huge tract of high and remote land which stretches away over the lofty crest of Black Edge before dropping gradually down to the outskirts of Buxton.

On the north-eastern slopes of this high moorland are two ancient but much-denuded burial mounds, Lady Low and Cow Low, but just a mile to the west, Castle Naze is one of the best preserved hillforts in the Peak District. It has probably been an important meeting place for our ancient ancestors for many thousands of years, but as yet no firm evidence has been found to confirm this. What is certain is that, in the later stages of the Bronze Age, its natural defences were added to when two great banks and ditches were constructed on the more gently sloping eastern slopes.

This walk begins in Combs, about seven hundred and fifty vertical feet below the ancient fort, yet only a mile away from it. For this reason it is not surprising that the quiet lane which climbs out of the village towards the hill rises very steeply. It passes over a small stream flowing past an old mill house and up past Castle Naze Farm to reach a high shoulder of the hill. Despite the steep incline, it is a pleasant lane overhung in places by tall trees, and bordered in the spring by a profusion of

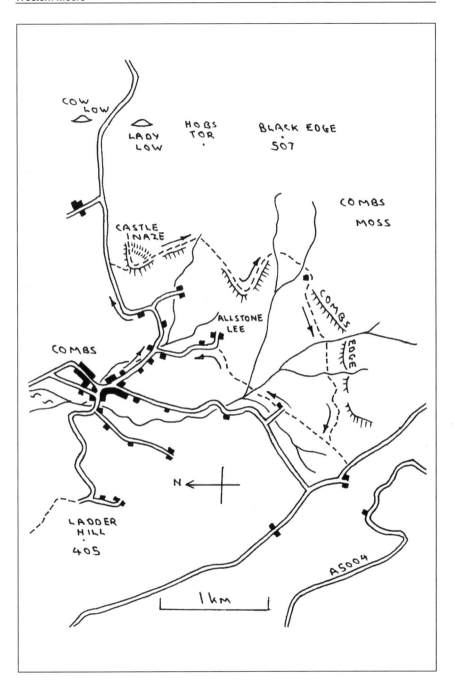

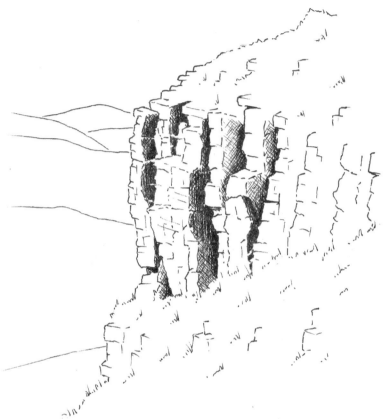

Natural defences of Castle Naze

forget-me-nots and pink campions. As the lane climbs the views gradually unfold, with Ladder Hill rising behind and in the far distance the darkly brooding bulk of Kinder Scout forming the horizon.

As the lane levels off, a footpath turns off to the right and climbs steeply straight up towards the towering cliffs of the hillfort now directly above. This path is used by the many rock climbers who can often be seen practicing their artistry on the fearsome crags, but it can also be followed up a wide and easy gully to reach the summit of the hill.

A path runs along the cliff edge in both directions, but if you follow the one to the left, running east, it soon brings you to a stile over a fence which gives access to the huge man-made defensive banks and the interior of the fort.

The banks run for about two hundred metres to link up with the natural cliffs along the other two sides of the triangular top. They are of similar height, although the outer one seems higher as it rises some fifteen feet above the bottom of the outer ditch which is much deeper than the inner one. In fact it has been cut down well below the level of the surrounding moor and often still holds standing water even in the driest periods.

The banks are made of earth mixed with the local slabby rock, which lies on top of the much solider rocks which form the cliffs below. Although mostly grassed over now, there are still a few places where the stones are exposed, showing how they have been laid horizontally with earth in between. Through the centre of the two banks is a deep-cut entrance running in from the south-east. The interior is generally flat with the exception of a small area near the high point where there are a series of hollows and hummocks.

No one really understands exactly why these hillforts were built, or how they were used by the local population. The theory that they were settlements that could be defended against warring neighbours is now being questioned, because there has been little actual evidence of fighting, or weapons or destruction found at most of them. Perhaps they were built more as symbols of power or importance, statements of ownership of the surrounding lands or as a focal point of a community or tribe. Perhaps they weren't really the refuge of the many but the seat of power of the few.

What is also clear is that the interior is too small for it to have been the permanent residence of a large community. Even as the home of a tribal leader it would have been very impractical. The difficulty of supplying a resident population with food and water over an extended period would have been anything but easy. Perhaps it was left empty and unused for large periods and used simply as a bolt-hole, an insurance policy in the event of an unexpected threat.

It would certainly have been a prominent and significant place that must have been seen from far way, and it could also look out over a huge tract of rich farmland. Even today, to stand above the great cliffs and look out over the Combs Valley spread out below, is to feel a sense of empowerment, of possession and of literally being above all else around.

From Castle Naze, a good path follows the top of the cliffs as they stretch away to the south. To the right, below the cliffs, a steep boulder field falls away to farmland, while off to the left is the wild heather moorland rising towards Black Edge. After a short distance the path traverses into a steep-sided clough, crosses over the tumbling stream in its bottom and climbs again out onto another promontory very similar to that of Castle Naze.

The path continues, following the cliff-line, all the time moving further and further away from the road and the few visitors to the fort who rarely progress far beyond it. This is wild country, and even the nearness of the farmland just below doesn't spoil the sense of isolation that can be found up there. The pristine moorland wilderness of Combs Moss stretches away beyond the cliffs of Combs Edge on the far side of the next deep clough. This is a largely trackless wilderness of heather and tussock grass and reeds. It acts like a great sponge, saturated by the heavy rainfall, feeding the many streams which radiate out from its centre. It is a grouse moor, and it is not uncommon to see these wonderful birds waddling comically away into the undergrowth, or hear their rattling, whirring cries as they clatter away in startled flight. Ravens perch on pinnacles of rock standing up above the steep bilberry-covered slopes and buzzards wheel on the rising air above the broken cliffs.

Eventually the path reaches an isolated shooting hut sitting beside one of the streams which cut down into the 'edge'. Although kept locked it does have a small open bothy beside it, where shelter could be

Man-made defences of Castle Naze

had in the event of bad weather. From the hut the path drops down onto the steep slopes below and traverses across the hillside.

This must once have been a good track as it is cut into the slope, but is now little used and in some parts can be overgrown and boggy. Despite these minor problems the scenery is tremendous and the peace and quiet priceless. At the bottom of the slope, the path winds across the hillside below the cliffs, but above the farmland. This is all 'Access land' and it is in places like this that the true benefits of these new rights can be appreciated. I saw stonechats perching precariously on sprigs of gorse, kestrels hanging in the sky, and in a steep gorge cutting deep into the hillside, clumps of beautiful wood-sorrel growing beside a tiny stream.

The path is narrow but easy to follow, until a stile is reached when it seems to vanish. Simply follow the line of the fence uphill until it reappears again, winding across the hillside below imposing cliffs. After another three or four hundred metres it joins a well-marked path dropping down the slope towards Broadlee Farm. The path skirts around the farm and across pleasant pastureland towards the next large farm of Allstone Lee. On the way it follows a line of very old, holed gateposts, and crosses two streams over footbridges. The first is wooden and recent, but the second is formed of a wonderful old, single gritstone slab with a handrail attached. On this return route the high spur of Castle Naze can be clearly seen, dominating the near skyline. From Allstone Lee a farm track runs back to the road, from where it is only a short distance back into Combs.

Most of the walks in this book can, if desired, be done in reverse. This one in particular is equally good in either direction. For those impatient to get to the hillfort quickly and put the steep ascent behind them, the route described is better. The alternative is a slow climb, first across the farmland then up onto the moors, before following the wild 'edge' along to reach Castle Naze. The advantage of this approach is that the hillfort is reached across a landscape much more similar to that of ancient times. In either direction this is a wonderful walk!

24. The Bullstones Wincle

Approx. distance: 6 miles

Approx. time: 3-4 hours

Starting point: Wincle GR 959661

Grade: A tricky walk, requiring some navigational skills, following well-marked but little used footpaths

O.S. Maps: Explorer sheet OL 24; Landranger sheet 118

Grid references: Wincle Minn standing stones GR 939659 and 940662; Cleulow Cross mound GR 952674; The Bullstones GR 956676; Cessbank Common tumulus GR 958681

On the western fringe of the Pennines, in the corner of Cheshire which is not completely flat, a great whaleback hill known as the Wincle Minn rises like a ramp into the hills of the Peak District. Along its length, and on the high col which links it to the hills beyond are a number of ancient sites which give us a remarkable insight into a Bronze Age community which once lived there.

When I last took this walk it was a wonderful clear Autumn day, but the fields were sodden and heavy with mud. The clear blue sky and the sharp wind scything over the open hills did their best to raise the spirit, but the energy-sapping mire beneath my feet eventually won the day. It is a walk for the late spring when the sun has climbed above the tree-tops, or the depths of Winter when the ground is firm beneath your boots.

It begins in Wincle, just a small church, a smaller school and a loose scattering of farms and houses on a high shelf above the deep valley of the River Dane. Starting from the church, the road to the south rises for a short way to where a footpath turns off to the right. Off to the left, the huge rocky prow of the Hangingstone can be clearly seen on the ridge climbing up towards the Roaches, with Hen Cloud beyond. The path climbs up and across the hillside to join a quiet lane beside the lovely old buildings of Wincle Grange.

Several paths leave the lane beside the house, but our route follows the drive, passing between the outbuildings before breaking out into

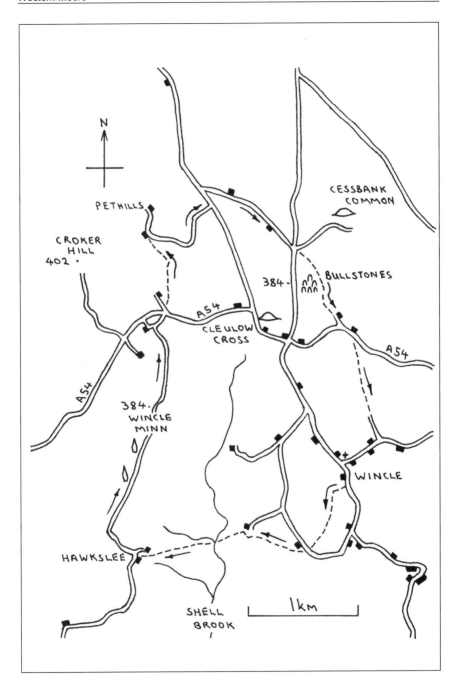

the fields. This is sheep country, with only the occasional gnarled remnants of redundant hawthorn hedges dividing the open pasture. The path drops gradually down towards the thickly wooded valley of Shell Brook, a line of stiles marking the way. After it passes to the left of an isolated farm it turns briefly to the right, back towards the farm, then drops steeply down a muddy track, passes through a gate and continues down to the banks of the stream.

A wooden bridge spans its shallow waters and from it a path climbs steeply up the wooded slopes beyond and over a stile to high open fields. These are quickly crossed, giving good views behind over the wooded valley below to the distant moors of the Peak. The path passes to the left of the new farm house, crosses a tiny bridge into the garden of Hawkslee and through it to reach the narrow Minn End Lane which climbs up towards the top of the Wincle Minn.

So far the route has offered little recompense to the weary walker, but now everything changes. The lane runs along the crest of the Minn with extensive views in all directions. To the west the Cheshire Plain sweeps away towards the Peckforton Hills, with the faint line of the Welsh Mountains beyond. To the north the striking summit cone of Shutlingsloe draws the eye. Away to the east the high heather moors of the Peak fade into the distance and to the south the isolated bulk of the Cloud stands darkly shadowed in the afternoon sunlight.

Minn is an ancient name, probably having the same origin as the welsh 'min' meaning edge and 'mynydd' meaning mountain, and probably predates both English and Welsh. It is even possible that the prehistoric people who walked its high ridge all those millennia ago called it by the same name!

Along its gently curving spine are a number of isolated gateposts, although the fields they once entered are now long gone. Three of these have been identified as Bronze Age standing stones, which in all probability once lined a trackway running along the hilltop. They are quite easily identified from the more recent additions by their marked lean and by their much smoother and more weathered appearance.

The first stands on its own, just to the left of the lane and leans drunkenly to the east. It is a four sided pillar which would originally have stood a little over four feet tall. About a hundred metres further on are two more upright, cleaner stones which are probably much more recent additions to the moor. Beyond them, again just to the left of the lane, are another pair. These two also lean, the first to the south and the

Wincle Minn standing stones

second to the west. Again they are just over four feet tall but unshaped and well-weathered.

If these are in fact ancient stones, which seems likely, are they in their original positions? If so, then these paired stones are an unusual monument in this area, although similar pairs are quite common in both Wales and the Lake District. Some, at least, of these pairs had cremation burials placed between the stones. Perhaps, like the nearby Bridestones, this site has more in common with the lands to the west than with the Peak District to the east. My gut feeling is that these were indeed waymarkers, spaced along the line of the ancient trackway running along the crest of the ridge, and that at least one of them has been moved to allow them to be used as gateposts when the hilltop was first enclosed.

Beyond the last of the stones the ridge rises to its highest point then drops gradually down towards the main road which passes over the high col beyond. Immediately across the road is a footpath, which drops down across field to meet an open bridleway leading to the lovely old farmhouse of Higher Pethills. From there, an unfenced lane runs eastwards.

When I last walked this way I disturbed several snipe which exploded startlingly from the wet fields beside the lane, and a mixed flock of redwings and fieldfares grazed on the berries which still hung in abundance on the bare branches of the hawthorns.

The Bullstones

Directly ahead, the distinctive shape of a large wooded mound rises above the line of the main road. This is Cleulow Cross. Now crowned by the ten foot tall remains of a wayside cross, it is reputedly an enormous prehistoric barrow. If so, it is one of the largest remaining tumuli in the whole of northern England!

The lane reaches a road, and a left and right turn takes you onto Withenshaw Lane, which climbs quickly back up into the hills. This then joins another lane, and from the junction two footpaths lead out onto the rolling fields of Cessbank Common beyond. The one to the left follows a track which leads past a Bronze Age barrow surmounted by a recent gravestone, but our route follows the one to the right. When the first stile is reached, the Bullstones appear on the skyline ahead and to the right. They sit in a slight dip below the highpoint of a spur of high ground rising from behind Cleulow Cross.

Classified as a stone circle, in fact the only remaining stone circle in Cheshire, this monument is a real enigma. It doesn't fit comfortably into any of the usual categories of ancient monuments, being neither a circle in the true sense nor a typical burial cairn. The Bullstones are a ring of low rounded stones about 9 paces across, some of which are now hidden beneath the grass. In the middle of the ring is a massive central stone surrounded by a loose pile of smaller stones. The central stone is only about four feet high but is broad and squat, giving an impression of solidity and permanence. Its top is well weathered and has a large solution hollow in its centre.

When excavated, a cremation burial was found within the ring, an upturned beaker buried about three feet below the surface containing the burnt bones of a child along with a flint arrowhead and knife.

Stone circles with large central stones are found in Scotland and Ireland and not too far away in Shropshire, but nowhere is such a large stone placed within such a small ring of tiny stones. It has also been suggested that it was once covered with a cairn and the ring of stones was a retaining kerb, but this seems unlikely. Another possibility is that the loose stones once formed a paved platform with the large stone in the centre. Something similar has been discovered near Llyn Brenig in North Wales.

Whatever the answer, it is a fascinating and very unusual monument, and like the neighbouring monuments seems to have little in common with those just a few miles to the east in the heart of the Peak District.

From the Bullstones, the path continues on, through the farmyard of Longgutter to the main road. This is followed for a short way to where another footpath turns off, opposite the pub, which soon joins a farm track, leading easily back into the village of Wincle.

Although the Bullstones are the only surviving monument in the near vicinity, with the possible exception of the Cleulow Cross mound, others were recorded in the 19th century. Another circle of stones once stood nearby and just to the south were a number of rings which were probably the remains of hut circles which have since been ploughed away.

Although some of the monuments which apparently survived until the last century have sadly now been lost, it seems clear that this area was once home to a thriving community. It is often difficult to be sure that such ancient monuments were all in use at the same time, but here we have a settlement, places of worship and burial, and a marked trackway linking them to the lands away to the west. It is interesting to speculate that these people perhaps had more in common with those far away places, as their monuments seem strangely out of place with the Peak District just over the hills to the east. Perhaps here, on the very fringe of the Pennines, lived people who had indeed come from the west, bringing with them a culture somewhat different to that of the indigenous population.

25. The Bridestones Rushton Spencer

Approx. distance: 6 miles

Approx. time: 3 hours

Starting point: Rushton Spencer GR 936625

Grade: An interesting and varied walk following footpaths and lanes over quiet farmland, high hills and peaceful river valleys. It visits one of the most spectacular megalithic sites in the whole area.

O.S. Maps: Explorer sheet 268; Landranger sheet 118

Grid references: The Bridestones GR 906622; The Cloud GR 905637

At the western edge of the Peak District, where the moorlands of Staffordshire drop down to meet the Cheshire Plain, a last bastion of the high gritstone plateau stands up above the town of Congleton. This is The Cloud, a high heather-clad edge rising as its name implies above the green fields below. Behind its sheer northern slopes it drops gently down to a high pass linking it to the hills behind. There, looking out over the plain towards the distant Welsh mountains, are the Bridestones, all that remain of a Neolithic chambered cairn of truly staggering proportions.

Our walk begins in Rushton Spencer, in a car park beside the old railway station on the now disused line from Macclesfield to Leek. It takes the lane westwards out of the village which climbs steeply up to the small cluster of houses and stone farm buildings at Rushton Bank. Here it leaves the road and branches off onto a little-used footpath which crosses high fields in the direction of the hamlet of Woodhouse Green.

The route is not always obvious, but the stiles are all there and the views are magnificent. Ahead is The Cloud, its sharp edged summit standing clear above its wooded slopes. Behind are all the hills of the western Peak, Croker Hill with its enormous radio mast, the long ridge of the Roaches, and shapely Shutlingsloe rising above the faint and distant line of Axe Edge. After a final rise, the path drops to meet a tiny lane at Oulton Manor which is quickly followed to Woodhouse Green. When

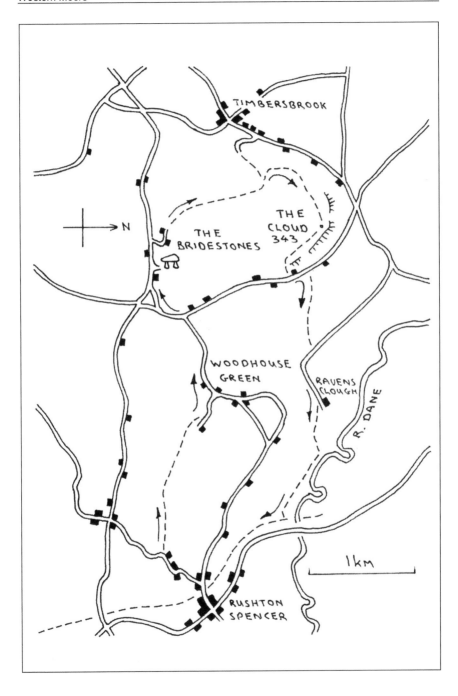

TIMBERSBROOK

→N

THE
CLOUD
343

THE
BRIDESTONES

WOODHOUSE
GREEN

RAVENS
CLOUGH

R. DANE

1km

RUSHTON
SPENCER

the fields are wet and the grass long, this same point can be reached with dry feet by simply following the lane all the way from Rushton Spencer.

The walk continues along the lane in the direction of The Cloud. Overhung by wizened oaks and majestic beeches, a tangled profusion of foxgloves and willowherb, brambles and cow parsley fringe the quiet road. I watched rabbits sitting in happy groups along the verge, a sparrowhawk gliding silently along the uncut hedgeline while in a tall oak a woodpecker hammered away on its hollow sounding post.

At the top of a steep slope another junction is reached and a left turn taken which runs alongside an area of mature woodland for just a short way until a right turn takes you into the wood.

This is a landscape that our Neolithic ancestors would have recognised, mature woodland of oak with an understorey of birch and rowan above a ground cover of ferns and brambles. Alive with birds and other wildlife, this small area is unfortunately just a tiny remnant of the great forest which once covered much of this area.

At the far side of the wood is a busier road which is followed for just a short way past the impressive house and gardens of Bridestones to reach the ancient monument of the same name. It can be clearly seen from the road but is reached along the driveway to the farm, now used by the Bridestones Stone company, where a gate gives access to the site.

Although much damaged and reduced from its original glory, the stones are still truly impressive. Two tall forecourt stones stand over ten feet tall, with another of almost six feet standing some distance away on the edge of the woods. They guard a long chamber formed from enormous slabs of stone which is blocked at the far end by a further tall upright. The side slabs join together almost perfectly, indicating that they were originally single huge slabs which have since broken. Several other large stones lie around the site, including what could be a capping stone near the entrance and a low slab which divides the chamber into two. When first recorded this dividing stone was much larger and had a porthole cut through it to give access into the rear part of the chamber.

The area outside the forecourt was still partly paved and traces of charcoal indicated that ritual fires might once have been lit there. It was also recorded that originally there were two further chambers, but that these were destroyed for use as building stone. The covering cairn was also said to be over a hundred yards in length which, even if an exaggeration, makes it one of the largest known, and on a similar scale to the

Forecourt stone at the Bridestones

great long barrow at West Kennet in Wiltshire. The cairn has almost entirely disappeared now, and the exposed stones now exhibit a wonderful mosaic of green and grey mosses and lichens partly covering the surface of the rich brown rock

What a sight it must have been, on the high pass looking out over the Cheshire plain to the Peckforton Hills and the distant Welsh Mountains. It almost certainly stood beside an ancient trackway which ran from the heart of the Peak District along the Knutsford Ridge to the Mersey Valley with its links by sea to Ireland. Perhaps it is not so surprising to find that in Northern Ireland there are many cairns of very similar construction to this one.

The stones are enclosed now in a small area between a field wall and a thick woodland of birch, pine and rhododendrons, so it is difficult to appreciate how large and imposing it must once have been, and also what a feat of organisation must have been required to construct such a gigantic tomb. No records remain of what was found within the chamber, but judging from the evidence found in cairns of a similar type it probably dates from as far back as 2700 BC.

To continue the walk, return to the road and follow it past the old Smithy Cottage to a right turn which quickly brings you back to the line of the long cairn trailing away from the burial chamber. The lane turns and passes a natural spring which must once have been very close to the tail of the cairn. This is significant as many Neolithic burial sites were indeed built close to, or sometimes over, already sacred springs. Perhaps these places, where life-giving water emerged from the ground, allowed the souls of the dead to return to the Mother Earth, in a similar way that caves were seen as entrances to the 'after life'.

The lane turns to a sandy bridleway which contours around the side of the hill, passing stands of spectacular Himalayan balsam growing beside the track and through an avenue of tall beech trees to reach an area of thicker woodland. Here a path forks off to the right, climbing quickly to reach the main trail up the Cloud, which weaves through a lovely woodland of stunted oaks, silver birch and Scot's pine. It eventually breaks out onto open moorland of heather and bilberry which rises gently to the summit, perched above the steep northern slopes looking out over the plain below. The Cloud really is the very edge of the Pennines, a last promontory of high ground thrusting like a ships prow into the green sea of Cheshire.

Five thousand years ago, when the builders of the Bridestones had stood here, they must have looked over an endless expanse of forest

The Bridestones

spreading out in all directions, only the distant Welsh mountains rising as a faint and purple rim on the far horizon. Even today the first impression is one of a green and well-wooded landscape rolling away into the distance, but they must have seen a wilderness unlike anything we can imagine today.

Just below the top, a line of low cliffs ring the edge of the plateau and the path follows along above these, descending gradually until a set of steep steps takes you down to a farm track leading back to the road. Turning left, the lane is followed for a short way to where a footpath drops steeply down to the right. Ahead is the tall radio mast on Croker Hill, beyond which the higher moors spread away to the north and east. The path crosses a boggy stretch over a series of very handy duckboards and enters an area of open parkland falling steeply away towards the Dane Valley below. The path meets a lane which is followed to the isolated farm at Raven Clough, from where a path leads you down into a steep-sided wooded dell dropping down to the main river valley.

The River Dane winds languidly between tree-lined banks, herons stalk in its shallows and cattle graze in scenes more reminiscent of a Constable painting than modern times. When I last walked along these banks I stopped to watch dozens of sand martens swooping and swirling in great circles beneath an old oak tree completely oblivious of my presence. The river at this point takes a great loop, and on the far side above a narrow shingle bay, tiny tell-tale holes in the steep sandy banks marked the site of their colony.

The path follows the river for a short way until a prominent post marks where it turns away, climbing gently before crossing a small tributary over a bridge made from a single slab of stone. Just beyond this is the embankment of a disused railway line, which is followed pleasantly back into Rushton Spencer.

Glossary of Technical terms

Avenue: a ceremonial route lined with paired standing stones, often linking stone circles with places of burial.

Barrow: an earthen mound covering a burial, usually round in shape.

Bronze Age: the period following the introduction of metal production. About 2 000 BC to 800 BC.

Cairn: a mound of stones, often covering a burial, usually round in shape.

Cairn circle: a cairn, of which only the kerb stones remain.

Capstone: the stone which forms the roof of a burial chamber or cist.

Causewayed camp: a Neolithic enclosure with many entrances, which may have been seasonal meeting places.

Chambered cairn: a cairn with a burial chamber, or chambers, inside it.

Chert: a local form of flint which could be made into sharp blades and tools.

Cist: a stone sarcophagus, usually found within or beneath a cairn or barrow.

Clearance cairn: a cairn made up of stones cleared from land on which crops were raised, and not usually associated with burial.

Enclosure: an area enclosed with prehistoric banks or ditches.

Forecourt: a stone-lined entrance to a chambered cairn or long barrow.

Henge: a circular enclosure surrounded by a bank that sometimes has an interior ditch.

Hillfort: a hilltop site defended by banks and ditches and dating from the late Bronze or Iron Age.

Iron Age: the period following the introduction of iron smelting. About 800 BC to the Roman conquest.

Kerb cairn: a burial cairn where the smaller cairn stones are held in place by larger kerb stones around the base.

Kerb stones: a ring of larger stones which hold in the smaller stones of a cairn.

Long barrow: a long mound, usually dating from the Neolithic period, usually with burial chambers inside.

Long cairn: a long cairn, usually with burial chambers inside.

Low: a local name for a burial mound or cairn

Megalith: a large stone, erected or positioned by Man in the Neolithic or Bronze Ages.

Mesolithic: the Middle Stone Age. The period following the Ice Age when early man lived as hunters and gatherers. About 8 000 BC to 4 000 BC.

Microliths: small stone tools and blades, usually made from flakes struck from flint or chert, dating from the Mesolithic period.

Neolithic: the New Stone Age. The period during which man changed from hunting and gathering to farming. About 4 000 BC to 2 000 BC.

Outlier: a standing stone positioned outside a stone circle.

Palaeolithic: the Old Stone Age. The period before the last Ice Age came to an end. It ended about 8 000 BC.

Prehistory: the era before the Roman conquest, which can be sub-divided into the Stone Age, the Bronze Age and the Iron Age.

Ringcairn: a ring of small stones or a circular stone bank with a level space inside and often with one or more entrances.

Rock shelter: a shallow cave or overhang used by early man.

Standing stone: stones which do not form part of a stone circle. May have been waymarkers or portals.

Stone circles: a circular ring of upright stones, sometimes built into a low bank.

Tumulus: an old name for a barrow.

Bibliography

A Gazetteer of English Caves, Fissures and Rock Shelters, A. Chamberlain and J. Williams, www.shef.ac.uk

The Megalithic Portal and Megalithic Map, www. megalithic.co.uk

Circles of Stone, Aubrey Burl, Harvill (1999)

Megaliths, David Corio and Lai Ngan Corio, Jonathan Cape (2003)

Prehistoric Cheshire, Victoria and Paul Morgan, Landmark (2004)

Prehistoric Art, T.G.E. Powell, Thames and Hudson (1966)

Prehistory in the Peak, Mark Edmonds and Tim Seaborne, Tempus (2001)

The Burial Mounds of Derbyshire, Barry Marsden (1994)

The Modern Antiquarian, Julian Cope, Thorsons (1998)